NorthStar 3
LISTENING & SPEAKING
FOURTH EDITION

Authors   HELEN S. SOLÓRZANO

JENNIFER P. L. SCHMIDT

Series Editors   FRANCES BOYD

CAROL NUMRICH

NorthStar: Listening & Speaking Level 3, Fourth Edition

Pearson Education, 10 Bank Street, White Plains, NY 10606

Staff credits: The people who made up the **NorthStar: Listening & Speaking Level 3, Fourth Edition** team, representing editorial, production, design, and manufacturing, are Kimberly Casey, Tracey Cataldo, Rosa Chapinal, Aerin Csigay, Mindy DePalma, Dave Dickey, Niki Lee, Françoise Leffler, Amy McCormick, Mary Perrotta Rich, Robert Ruvo, and Debbie Sistino

Text composition: ElectraGraphics, Inc.
Editorial: Goathaus Studio and Wildwood Ink

Library of Congress Cataloging-in-Publication Data

Frazier, Laurie.
  Northstar 2 : Listening and speaking / Authors : Laurie Frazier, Robin Mills. — Fourth Edition. /
Frazier, Laurie.
      pages cm
  ISBN-13: 978-0-13-338213-6 (Level 2) – ISBN 978-0-13-294040-5 (Level 3) – ISBN 978-0-13-338207-5
(Level 4) – ISBN 978-0-13-338214-3 (Level 5)
1. English language—Textbooks for foreign speakers. 2. English language—Spoken English—Problems, exercises, etc. 3. Listening—Problems, exercises, etc. I. Mills, Robin, 1962– II. Title. III. Title: Northstar two. IV. Title: Listening and speaking.
  PE1128.M586 2015
  428.2'4—dc23
                                                                                    2013050585

Printed in the United States of America

ISBN 10: 0-13-294040-X
ISBN 13: 978-0-13-294040-5

5 18

ISBN 10: 0-13-404981-0 (International Edition)
ISBN 13: 978-0-13-404981-6 (International Edition)

CONTENTS

WELCOME TO NORTHSTAR

A BLENDED-LEARNING COURSE FOR THE 21ST CENTURY

Building on the success of previous editions, *NorthStar* continues to engage and motivate students through new and updated contemporary, authentic topics in a seamless integration of print and online content. Students will achieve their academic as well as language and personal goals in order to meet the challenges of the 21st century.

New for the FOURTH EDITION

★ Fully Blended MyEnglishLab

NorthStar aims to prepare students for academic success and digital literacy with its fully blended online lab. The innovative new MyEnglishLab: *NorthStar* gives learners immediate feedback—anytime, anywhere—as they complete auto-graded language activities online.

★ NEW and UPDATED THEMES

Current and thought-provoking topics presented in a variety of genres promote intellectual stimulation. The authentic content engages students, links them to language use outside of the classroom, and encourages personal expression and critical thinking.

★ EXPLICIT SKILL INSTRUCTION and PRACTICE

Language skills are highlighted in each unit, providing students with systematic and multiple exposures to language forms and structures in a variety of contexts. Concise presentations and targeted practice in print and online prepare students for academic success.

★ LEARNING OUTCOMES and ASSESSMENT

A variety of assessment tools, including online diagnostic, formative, and summative assessments, and a flexible gradebook, aligned with clearly identified unit learning outcomes allow teachers to individualize instruction and track student progress.

THE NORTHSTAR APPROACH TO CRITICAL THINKING

What is critical thinking?

Most textbooks include interesting questions for students to discuss and tasks for students to engage in to develop language skills. And often these questions and tasks are labeled critical thinking. Look at this question as an example:

When you buy fruits and vegetables, do you usually look for the cheapest price? Explain.

The question may inspire a lively discussion with students exploring a variety of viewpoints—but it doesn't necessarily develop critical thinking. Now look at another example:

When people in your neighborhood buy fruits and vegetables, what factors are the most important: the price, the freshness, locally grown, organic (without chemicals)? Make a prediction and explain. How can you find out if your prediction is correct? This question does develop critical thinking. It asks students to make predictions, formulate a hypothesis, and draw a conclusion—all higher-level critical thinking skills. Critical thinking, as philosophers and psychologists suggest, is a sharpening and a broadening of the mind. A critical thinker engages in true problem solving, connects information in novel ways, and challenges assumptions. A critical thinker is a skillful, responsible thinker who is open-minded and has the ability to evaluate information based on evidence. Ultimately, through this process of critical thinking, students are better able to decide what to think, what to say, or what to do.

How do we teach critical thinking?

It is not enough to teach "about" critical thinking. Teaching the theory of critical thinking will not produce critical thinkers. Additionally, it is not enough to simply expose students to good examples of critical thinking without explanation or explicit practice and hope our students will learn by imitation.

Students need to engage in specially designed exercises that aim to improve critical-thinking skills. This approach practices skills both implicitly and explicitly and is embedded in thought-provoking content. Some strategies include:

- subject matter that is carefully selected and exploited so that students learn new concepts and encounter new perspectives.
- students identifying their own assumptions about the world and later challenging them.
- activities that are designed in a way that students answer questions and complete language-learning tasks that may not have black-and-white answers. (Finding THE answer is often less valuable than the process by which answers are derived.)
- activities that engage students in logical thinking, where they support their reasoning and resolve differences with their peers.

Infused throughout each unit of each book, *NorthStar* uses the principles and strategies outlined above, including:

- Make Inferences: inference comprehension questions in every unit
- Vocabulary and Comprehension: categorization activities
- Vocabulary and Synthesize: relationship analyses (analogies); comparisons (Venn diagrams)
- Synthesize: synthesis of information from two texts teaches a "multiplicity" approach rather than a "duality" approach to learning; ideas that seem to be in opposition on the surface may actually intersect and reinforce each other
- Focus on the Topic and Preview: identifying assumptions, recognizing attitudes and values, and then re-evaluating them
- Focus on Writing/Speaking: reasoning and argumentation
- Unit Project: judgment; choosing factual, unbiased information for research projects
- Focus on Writing/Speaking and Express Opinions: decision-making; proposing solutions

THE NORTHSTAR UNIT

1 FOCUS ON THE TOPIC

* **CT** Each unit begins with a photo that draws students into the topic. Focus questions motivate students and encourage them to make personal connections. Students make inferences about and predict the content of the unit.

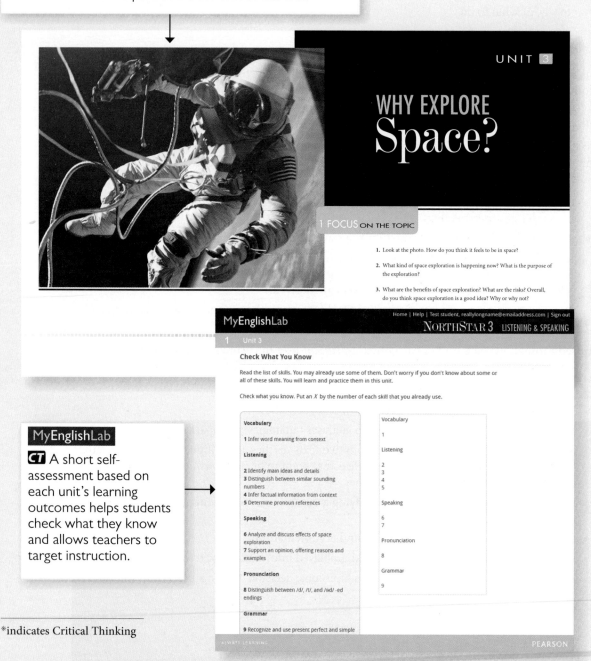

UNIT 3

WHY EXPLORE Space?

1 FOCUS ON THE TOPIC

1. Look at the photo. How do you think it feels to be in space?

2. What kind of space exploration is happening now? What is the purpose of the exploration?

3. What are the benefits of space exploration? What are the risks? Overall, do you think space exploration is a good idea? Why or why not?

MyEnglishLab

Home | Help | Test student, reallylongname@emailaddress.com | Sign out

NORTHSTAR 3 LISTENING & SPEAKING

1 Unit 3

Check What You Know

Read the list of skills. You may already use some of them. Don't worry if you don't know about some or all of these skills. You will learn and practice them in this unit.

Check what you know. Put an *X* by the number of each skill that you already use.

Vocabulary	Vocabulary
1 Infer word meaning from context	1
Listening	Listening
2 Identify main ideas and details	2
3 Distinguish between similar sounding numbers	3
4 Infer factual information from context	4
5 Determine pronoun references	5
Speaking	Speaking
6 Analyze and discuss effects of space exploration	6
7 Support an opinion, offering reasons and examples	7
Pronunciation	Pronunciation
8 Distinguish between /d/, /t/, and /əd/ -ed endings	8
Grammar	Grammar
9 Recognize and use present perfect and simple	9

ALWAYS LEARNING

PEARSON

MyEnglishLab

CT A short self-assessment based on each unit's learning outcomes helps students check what they know and allows teachers to target instruction.

---

*indicates Critical Thinking

2 FOCUS ON LISTENING

Two contrasting, thought-provoking listening selections, from a variety of authentic genres, stimulate students intellectually.

CT Students predict content, verify their predictions, and follow up with a variety of tasks that ensure comprehension.

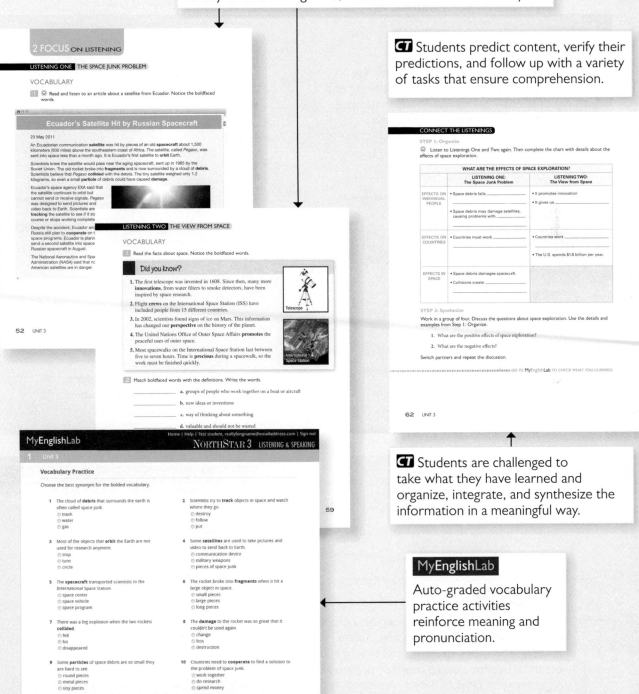

2 FOCUS ON LISTENING

LISTENING ONE | THE SPACE JUNK PROBLEM

VOCABULARY

1. Read and listen to an article about a satellite from Ecuador. Notice the boldfaced words.

Ecuador's Satellite Hit by Russian Spacecraft

23 May 2011

An Ecuadorian communication **satellite** was hit by pieces of an old **spacecraft** about 1,500 kilometers (930 miles) above the southeastern coast of Africa. The satellite, called *Pegaso*, was sent into space less than a month ago. It is Ecuador's first satellite to **orbit** Earth.

Scientists knew the satellite would pass near the aging spacecraft, sent up in 1985 by the Soviet Union. The old rocket broke into **fragments** and is now surrounded by a cloud of **debris**. Scientists believe that *Pegaso* **collided** with the debris. The tiny satellite weighed only 1.2 kilograms, so even a small **particle** of debris could have caused **damage**.

Ecuador's space agency EXA said that the satellite continues to orbit but cannot send or receive signals. *Pegaso* was designed to send pictures and video back to Earth. Scientists are **tracking** the satellite to see if it stays on course or stops working completely.

Despite the accident, Ecuador and Russia still plan to **cooperate** on their space programs. Ecuador is planning to send a second satellite into space on a Russian spacecraft in August.

The National Aeronautics and Space Administration (NASA) said that no American satellites are in danger.

52   UNIT 3

LISTENING TWO | THE VIEW FROM SPACE

VOCABULARY

1. Read the facts about space. Notice the boldfaced words.

Did you know?

1. The first telescope was invented in 1608. Since then, many more **innovations**, from water filters to smoke detectors, have been inspired by space research.

Telescope

2. Flight **crews** on the International Space Station (ISS) have included people from 15 different countries.

3. In 2002, scientists found signs of ice on Mars. This information has changed our **perspective** on the history of the planet.

4. The United Nations Office of Outer Space Affairs **promotes** the peaceful uses of outer space.

International Space Station

5. Most spacewalks on the International Space Station last between five to seven hours. Time is **precious** during a spacewalk, so the work must be finished quickly.

2. Match boldfaced words with the definitions. Write the words.

_____ a. groups of people who work together on a boat or aircraft

_____ b. new ideas or inventions

_____ c. way of thinking about something

_____ d. valuable and should not be wasted

CONNECT THE LISTENINGS

STEP 1: Organize

Listen to Listenings One and Two again. Then complete the chart with details about the effects of space exploration.

WHAT ARE THE EFFECTS OF SPACE EXPLORATION?		
	LISTENING ONE: The Space Junk Problem	**LISTENING TWO:** The View from Space
EFFECTS ON INDIVIDUAL PEOPLE	• Space debris falls _____ • Space debris may damage satellites, causing problems with _____	• It promotes innovation • It gives us _____
EFFECTS ON COUNTRIES	• Countries must work _____	• Countries work _____ • The U.S. spends $1.8 billion per year.
EFFECTS IN SPACE	• Space debris damages spacecraft. • Collisions create _____	

STEP 2: Synthesize

Work in a group of four. Discuss the questions about space exploration. Use the details and examples from Step 1: Organize.

1. What are the positive effects of space exploration?

2. What are the negative effects?

Switch partners and repeat the discussion.

GO TO MyEnglishLab TO CHECK WHAT YOU LEARNED.

62   UNIT 3

CT Students are challenged to take what they have learned and organize, integrate, and synthesize the information in a meaningful way.

MyEnglishLab

Home | Help | Test student, reallylongname@emailaddress.com | Sign out

NORTHSTAR 3 LISTENING & SPEAKING

Unit 3

Vocabulary Practice

Choose the best synonym for the bolded vocabulary.

1. The cloud of **debris** that surrounds the earth is often called space junk.
   - trash
   - water
   - gas

2. Scientists try to **track** objects in space and watch where they go.
   - destroy
   - follow
   - put

3. Most of the objects that **orbit** the Earth are not used for research anymore.
   - stop
   - turn
   - circle

4. Some **satellites** are used to take pictures and video to send back to Earth.
   - communication device
   - military weapons
   - pieces of space junk

5. The **spacecraft** transported scientists to the International Space Station.
   - space center
   - space vehicle
   - space program

6. The rocket broke into **fragments** when it hit a large object in space.
   - small pieces
   - large pieces
   - long pieces

7. There was a big explosion when the two rockets **collided**.
   - fell
   - hit
   - disappeared

8. The **damage** to the rocket was so great that it couldn't be used again.
   - change
   - loss
   - destruction

9. Some **particles** of space debris are so small they are hard to see.
   - round pieces
   - metal pieces
   - tiny pieces

10. Countries need to **cooperate** to find a solution to the problem of space junk.
    - work together
    - do research
    - spend money

59

ALWAYS LEARNING   PEARSON

MyEnglishLab

Auto-graded vocabulary practice activities reinforce meaning and pronunciation.

EXPLICIT SKILL INSTRUCTION AND PRACTICE

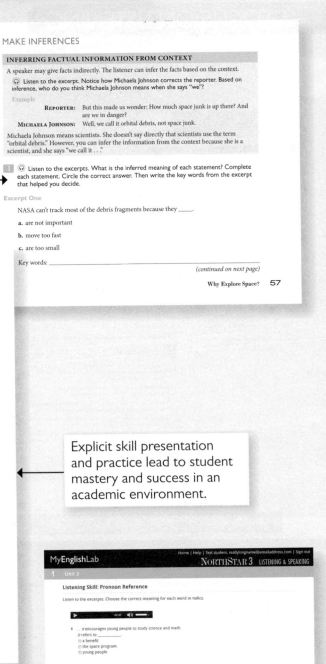

MAKE INFERENCES

INFERRING FACTUAL INFORMATION FROM CONTEXT

A speaker may give facts indirectly. The listener can infer the facts based on the context.

🎧 Listen to the excerpt. Notice how Michaela Johnson corrects the reporter. Based on inference, who do you think Michaela Johnson means when she says "we"?

Example

REPORTER: But this made us wonder: How much space junk is up there? And are we in danger?

MICHAELA JOHNSON: Well, we call it orbital debris, not space junk.

Michaela Johnson means scientists. She doesn't say directly that scientists use the term "orbital debris." However, you can infer the information from the context because she is a scientist, and she says "we call it . . ."

1 🎧 Listen to the excerpts. What is the inferred meaning of each statement? Complete each statement. Circle the correct answer. Then write the key words from the excerpt that helped you decide.

Excerpt One

NASA can't track most of the debris fragments because they _____.

a. are not important

b. move too fast

c. are too small

Key words: _____

(continued on next page)

CT Step-by-step instructions and practice guide students to exercise critical thinking and to dig deeper by asking questions that move beyond the literal meaning of the text.

LISTENING SKILL

1 🎧 Listen to an excerpt from the interview with Ray Santos. What does the word *it* refer to?

Is **it** worth the price?

PRONOUN REFERENCE

Speakers use pronouns (*it, they, this, that, he, she*) to refer to people, things, and ideas. It is important to understand which people, things, or ideas a speaker is referring to.

A pronoun may refer to something mentioned before or to an idea that is not directly stated.

🎧 Listen to the excerpt. Notice the pronouns in **bold**.

Example

RAY SANTOS: Space exploration has a lot of benefits. One is innovation. The research for the space program has led to all kinds of innovations.

INTERVIEWER: Can you tell us about some of **those**?

RAY SANTOS: Think about **it**: To get into space **we** had to solve all kinds of problems.

- **Those** refers to *innovations*.
- **It** refers to *space exploration*.
- **We** refers to *scientists or people in general*.

2 🎧 Listen to the excerpts. Then write the meaning of the boldfaced words.

Pronoun	Refers to
Excerpt One	
a. *It* has brought together international flight crews	it = _____
b. *This cooperation* promotes positive relationships	this cooperation = cooperation between _____
Excerpt Two	
c. *we*'ve had a great curiosity	we = _____
d. *This curiosity* has led us to explore	this curiosity = curiosity about _____
e. And *it* doesn't just give us answers —*it* gives perspective	it = _____
f. we see how precious *it* is . . .	it = _____

═══════════════ GO TO MyEnglishLab *FOR MORE SKILL PRACTICE.*

Explicit skill presentation and practice lead to student mastery and success in an academic environment.

MyEnglishLab

Key listening skills are reinforced and practiced in new contexts. Meaningful and instant feedback provides students and teachers with essential information to monitor progress.

Using models from the unit listening selections, the pronunciation and speaking skill sections expose students to the sounds and patterns of English as well as to functional language that prepares them to express ideas on a higher level.

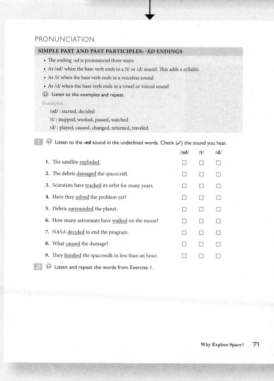

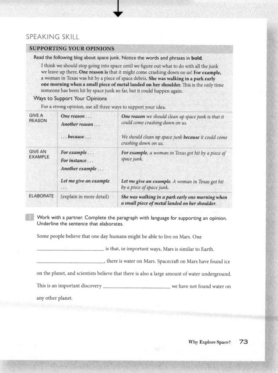

FOCUS ON SPEAKING

Productive vocabulary targeted in the unit is reviewed, expanded upon, and used creatively in this section and in the final speaking task. Grammar structures useful for the final speaking task are presented and practiced. A concise grammar skills box serves as an excellent reference.

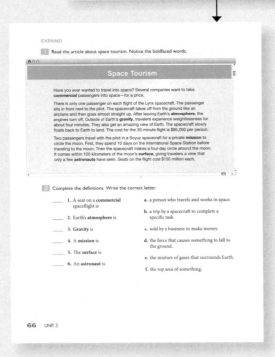

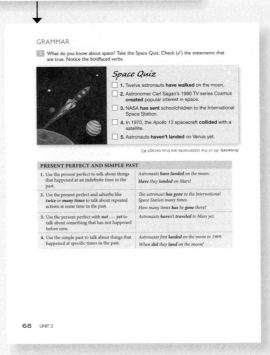

MyEnglishLab

Auto-graded vocabulary and grammar practice activities with feedback reinforce meaning, form, and function.

CT A final speaking task gives students an opportunity to exchange ideas and express opinions in sustained speaking contexts using vocabulary, grammar, pronunciation, listening, and speaking skills presented in the unit.

FINAL SPEAKING TASK

In a small group discussion, people share information and have a conversation about the ideas.

In this activity, you will have two small group discussions about the positive and negative effects of space exploration.

Work in groups. Follow the steps. Try to use the vocabulary, grammar, pronunciation, and listening and speaking skills that you learned in the unit.*

STEP 1: Divide into four groups. Each group will read and discuss the information for *one* of the following topics about the U.S. space program (Student Activities, page 211):

- Finance and Economy
- Environment
- Innovation and Development
- Human Relations

In your group:

1. Read only the information for your topic. (For example, if your topic is "Finance and Economy," read only the information in that section.)

2. Discuss the information and sort it into two categories. Label the information "Positive" or "Negative."

3. Add any other information that you know about your topic, and label it "Positive" or "Negative."

4. Be prepared to explain the information in your own words (without reading) in the next step.

STEP 2: Divide into four new groups. Each group should have an "expert" from one of the four topic areas (one person from Finance and Economy, Environment, Innovation and Development, and Human Relations). Present the information about your topic to the group. After each person presents, discuss the questions.

1. What are the positive effects of the space program?

2. What are the negative effects of the space program?

3. As a group, consider all the information and decide: Is space exploration a good idea? Why or why not?

———————————
*For Alternative Speaking Topics, see page 77.

Why Explore Space? 75

CT A group unit project inspires students to inquire further and prepares students to engage in real-world activities. Unit projects incorporate Internet research, helping to build students' digital literacy skills.

UNIT PROJECT

There are many exciting projects planned for future space exploration. Some are scientific projects planned by government space agencies, and others are commercial projects planned by private businesses.

STEP 1: Choose a space project to research. You can choose a project from the list below or another similar project.

SUGGESTED TOPICS

NASA Projects	Commercial Projects
Asteroid[1] Redirect Initiative	Asteroid Mining
Commercial Crew Program	Space Tourism
IRIS (Interface Region Imaging Spectograph)	Mars One
Mars 2020 Mission Plans	
LADEE (Lunar Atmosphere Dust Environment Explorer)	
International Space Station	

STEP 2: Research the project. Learn about the project by listening to an online lecture or report, visiting a science museum, visiting an educational website, or doing another type of research. Find out about the goals of the project and the plans for reaching the goals.

STEP 3: Prepare a presentation on the project for your class.

———————————
[1] **asteroid:** a small rocky object that orbits the sun

76 UNIT 3

INNOVATIVE TEACHING TOOLS

With instant access to a wide range of online content and diagnostic tools, teachers can customize learning environments to meet the needs of every student.

USING MyEnglishLab, NORTHSTAR TEACHERS CAN:

Deliver rich online content to engage and motivate students, including:

- student audio to support listening and speaking skills.
- engaging, authentic video clips, including reports adapted from ABC, NBC, and CBS newscasts, tied to the unit themes.
- opportunities for written and recorded reactions to be submitted by students.

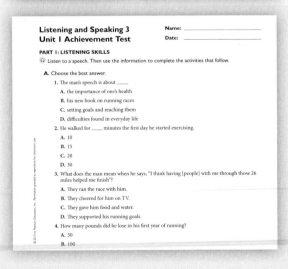

Use a powerful selection of diagnostic reports to:

- view student scores by unit, skill, and activity.
- monitor student progress on any activity or test as often as needed.
- analyze class data to determine steps for remediation and support.

Use Teacher Resource eText* to access:

- a digital copy of the student book for whole class instruction.
- downloadable achievement and placement tests.
- printable resources, including lesson planners, videoscripts, and video activities.
- classroom audio.
- unit teaching notes and answer keys.

* Teacher Resource eText is accessible through MyEnglishLab: *NorthStar*.

COMPONENTS   Print or eText

STUDENT BOOK and MyEnglishLab

★ Student Book with MyEnglishLab

The two strands, *Reading & Writing* and *Listening & Speaking,* for each of the five levels, provide a fully blended approach with the seamless integration of print and online content.

eTEXT and MyEnglishLab

★ eText with MyEnglishLab

Offering maximum flexibility for different learning styles and needs, a digital version of the student book can be used on iPad® and Android® devices.

★ Instructor Access: Teacher Resource eText and MyEnglishLab (Listening & Speaking 1–5)

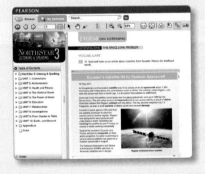

Teacher Resource eText

Each level and strand of *NorthStar* has an accompanying Teacher Resource eText that includes: a digital student book, unit teaching notes, answer keys, downloadable achievement tests, classroom audio, lesson planners, video activities, videoscripts, and a downloadable placement test.

MyEnglishLab

Teachers assign MyEnglishLab activities to reinforce the skills students learn in class and monitor progress through an online gradebook. The automatically graded exercises in MyEnglishLab *NorthStar* support and build on academic skills and vocabulary presented and practiced in the Student Book/eText. The teacher-graded activities include pronunciation, speaking, and writing, and are assigned by the instructor.

★ Classroom Audio CD

The Listening & Speaking audio contains the recordings and activities, as well as audio for the achievement tests. The Reading & Writing strand contains the readings on audio.

SCOPE AND SEQUENCE

UNIT OUTCOMES	1 EXTREME SPORTS **A TEST OF ENDURANCE** pages 2–27 *Listening 1: Ultrarunner: Jay Batchen* *Listening 2: Sports Psychology*	2 FRAUD **AVOIDING IDENTITY THEFT** pages 28–49 *Listening 1: Lily's Story* *Listening 2: Public Service Announcements*
LISTENING	• Make and confirm predictions • Identify main ideas and details • Recognize signal words that tell what to expect MyEnglishLab Vocabulary and Listening Skill Practice	• Make and confirm predictions • Identify main ideas and details • Recognize rhetorical questions MyEnglishLab Vocabulary and Listening Skill Practice
SPEAKING	• Ask for and express opinions • Support ideas in one listening with examples from another listening • Use appropriate language to agree and disagree **Task:** Interpret, discuss and create aphorisms MyEnglishLab Speaking Skill Practice and Speaking Task	• Ask for and give advice • Apply strategies to keep a conversation going **Task:** Create and dramatize a story about an experience with crime MyEnglishLab Speaking Skill Practice and Speaking Task
INFERENCE	• Infer meaning from context in a listening	• Infer a speaker's feelings from intonation and stress
PRONUNCIATION	• Recognize, use, and distinguish between expressions with *other (each other, another)* MyEnglishLab Pronunciation Skill Practice	• Identify stress and pitch patterns in common compound nouns MyEnglishLab Pronunciation Skill Practice
VOCABULARY	• Infer word meaning from context • Describe goals and challenges MyEnglishLab Vocabulary Practice	• Infer word meaning from context • Interpret positive and negative connotations of vocabulary words MyEnglishLab Vocabulary Practice
GRAMMAR	• Recognize and use reflexive and reciprocal pronouns MyEnglishLab Grammar Practice	• Recognize and use modals of advice MyEnglishLab Grammar Practice
VIDEO	MyEnglishLab *Danny Parks, BMX Pro*, Video Activity	MyEnglishLab *Unhappy Returns*, NBC News, Video Activity
ASSESSMENTS	MyEnglishLab Check What You Know, Checkpoints I and 2, Unit I Achievement Test	MyEnglishLab Check What You Know, Checkpoints I and 2, Unit 2 Achievement Test

3 SPACE
WHY EXPLORE SPACE?
pages 50–77

Listening 1: The Space Junk Problem
Listening 2: The View from Space

4 LANGUAGE
WORDS THAT PERSUADE
pages 78–103

Listening 1: Corporate Euphemisms
Listening 2: House Hunting

• Make and confirm predictions • Identify main ideas and details • Distinguish between similar sounding numbers • Determine pronoun references **MyEnglishLab** Vocabulary and Listening Skill Practice	• Make and confirm predictions • Identify main ideas and details • Recognize intensifiers that emphasize ideas **MyEnglishLab** Vocabulary and Listening Skill Practice
• Analyze and categorize effects • Support ideas with details and examples **Task:** Discuss opinions about effects of space exploration, offering reasons and examples **MyEnglishLab** Speaking Skill Practice and Speaking Task	• Use language strategies to appeal to emotions • Express a point of view **Task:** Create and dramatize a persuasive advertisement **MyEnglishLab** Speaking Skill Practice and Speaking Task
• Infer factual information from context	• Infer a speaker's purpose
• Distinguish between /d/, /t/, and /əd/ endings **MyEnglishLab** Pronunciation Skill Practice	• Recognize and use intonation and stress for emphasis **MyEnglishLab** Pronunciation Skill Practice
• Infer word meaning from context **MyEnglishLab** Vocabulary Practice	• Infer word meaning from context • Categorize common words and phrases in advertisements **MyEnglishLab** Vocabulary Practice
• Recognize and use present perfect and simple past **MyEnglishLab** Grammar Practice	• Recognize and use superlative adjectives **MyEnglishLab** Grammar Practice
MyEnglishLab *Life in Space,* ABC News, Video Activity	**MyEnglishLab** *Gender and Communication,* Insight Media Video Activity
MyEnglishLab Check What You Know, Checkpoints 1 and 2, Unit 3 Achievement Test	**MyEnglishLab** Check What You Know, Checkpoints 1 and 2, Unit 4 Achievement Test

SCOPE AND SEQUENCE

UNIT OUTCOMES	5 CAREERS **FOLLOW YOUR PASSION** pages 104–127 *Listening 1: Changing Career Paths* *Listening 2: Finding Your Passion*	6 TOURISM **CULTURE AND COMMERCE** pages 128–153 *Listening 1: Tourist Attraction or Human Zoo?* *Listening 2: Town Hall Meeting in Cape Cod*
LISTENING	• Make and confirm predictions • Identify main ideas and details • Recognize common reductions in speech **MyEnglishLab** Vocabulary and Listening Skill Practice	• Make and confirm predictions • Identify main ideas and details • Recognize markers that signal an opinion **MyEnglishLab** Vocabulary and Listening Skill Practice
SPEAKING	• Ask for and give advice • Use follow-up questions to extend conversation, ask for clarification, or gain information **Task:** Create and dramatize a job interview **MyEnglishLab** Speaking Skill Practice and Speaking Task	• Evaluate and debate the effects of tourism • Use expressions to make suggestions and give advice **Task:** Participate in a simulation: Defend and support a proposal **MyEnglishLab** Speaking Skill Practice and Speaking Task
INFERENCE	• Infer meaning from context in a listening	• Infer a speaker's attitude and emotion from word choice
PRONUNCIATION	• Distinguish between rising and falling intonation in questions **MyEnglishLab** Pronunciation Skill Practice	• Distinguish between different pronunciations and spellings for the letter *o* **MyEnglishLab** Pronunciation Skill Practice
VOCABULARY	• Infer word meaning from context **MyEnglishLab** Vocabulary Practice	• Infer word meaning from context • Categorize words with similar meanings **MyEnglishLab** Vocabulary Practice
GRAMMAR	• Recognize and use infinitives of purpose **MyEnglishLab** Grammar Practice	• Recognize and make predictions using *will* and *if* clauses **MyEnglishLab** Grammar Practice
VIDEO	**MyEnglishLab** *Dream Jobs,* ABC News Video Activity	**MyEnglishLab** *The Benefits of Ecotourism,* Video Activity
ASSESSMENTS	**MyEnglishLab** Check What You Know, Checkpoints 1 and 2, Unit 5 Achievement Test	**MyEnglishLab** Check What You Know, Checkpoints 1 and 2, Unit 6 Achievement Test

7 MARRIAGE
BEFORE YOU SAY "I DO"
pages 154–179
Listening 1: A Prenuptial Agreement
Listening 2: Reactions to the Prenuptial Agreement

8 CLIMATE CHANGE
REDUCING YOUR CARBON FOOTPRINT
pages 180–209
Listening 1: Living Small
Listening 2: A Call to Action

• Make and confirm predictions • Identify main ideas and details • Identify reasons for a speaker's opinion • Recognize markers that signal disagreement and a contrasting opinion MyEnglishLab Vocabulary and Listening Skill Practice	• Make and confirm predictions • Identify main ideas and details • Interpret statistics in order to label a graph • Recognize repetition of ideas to emphasize key points MyEnglishLab Vocabulary and Listening Skill Practice
• Evaluate advantages and disadvantages and debate a position • Use transitions when making oral presentations **Task:** Prepare and present an oral report MyEnglishLab Speaking Skill Practice and Speaking Task	• Use expressions to agree and disagree • Use strategies to interrupt politely and hold the floor • Use strategies to lead a discussion **Task:** Participate in an academic seminar MyEnglishLab Speaking Skill Practice and Speaking Task
• Infer certainty from word choice	• Infer contrast based on context
• Recognize and use contrastive stress for emphasis MyEnglishLab Pronunciation Skill Practice	• Identify whether a speaker is pausing or concluding based on intonation MyEnglishLab Pronunciation Skill Practice
• Infer word meaning from context MyEnglishLab Vocabulary Practice	• Infer word meaning from context • Recognize and use word forms (nouns, verbs, adjectives) MyEnglishLab Vocabulary Practice
• Recognize and use comparatives and equatives with adjectives and adverbs MyEnglishLab Grammar Practice	• Recognize and use modals of necessity in the present and future MyEnglishLab Grammar Practice
MyEnglishLab *Couples Protect Themselves with Postnup,* ABC News, Video Activity	MyEnglishLab *Living the Real Simple Life,* ABC News Video Activity
MyEnglishLab Check What You Know, Checkpoints 1 and 2, Unit 7 Achievement Test	MyEnglishLab Check What You Know, Checkpoints 1 and 2, Unit 8 Achievement Test

ACKNOWLEDGMENTS

It has been a pleasure to work with the many dedicated people who supported the creation of this book. Special thanks go to Frances Boyd and Carol Numrich for their vision and guidance and to our editorial team for their feedback and support.

We would like to dedicate this edition of *NorthStar* to Debbie Sistino for her support and the skilled editorial insights that have enriched our work.

Many thanks to producers Tim Borquin, Erik Michielsen and Alison Grayson for their creative and thought-provoking audio pieces and to Jay Batchen, "Lily" and Julia Brown (Peters) for sharing their stories.

And finally, we thank our husbands, Roy Solórzano and David Schmidt, and our children, Alonzo, Lucia, Christina, and Andrew for their patience and support throughout the writing of this 4th edition.

—*Helen Solórzano and Jennifer Schmidt*

REVIEWERS

Chris Antonellis, Boston University – CELOP; Gail August, Hostos; Aegina Barnes, York College; Kim Bayer, Hunter College; Mine Bellikli, Atilim University; Allison Blechman, Embassy CES; Paul Blomquist, Kaplan; Helena Botros, FLS; James Branchick, FLS; Chris Bruffee, Embassy CES; Nese Cakli, Duzce University; María Cordani Tourinho Dantas, Colégio Rainha De Paz; Jason Davis, ASC English; Lindsay Donigan, Fullerton College; Bina Dugan, BCCC; Sibel Ece Izmir, Atilim University; Érica Ferrer, Universidad del Norte; María Irma Gallegos Peláez, Universidad del Valle de México; Jeff Gano, ASA College; María Genovev a Chávez Bazán, Universidad del Valle de México; Juan Garcia, FLS; Heidi Gramlich, The New England School of English; Phillip Grayson, Kaplan; Rebecca Gross, The New England School of English; Rick Guadiana, FLS; Sebnem Guzel, Tobb University; Esra Hatipoglu, Ufuk University; Brian Henry, FLS; Josephine Horna, BCCC; Arthur Hui, Fullerton College; Zoe Isaacson, Hunter College; Kathy Johnson, Fullerton College; Marcelo Juica, Urban College of Boston; Tom Justice, North Shore Community College; Lisa Karakas, Berkeley College; Eva Kopernacki, Embassy CES; Drew Larimore, Kaplan; Heidi Lieb, BCCC; Patricia Martins, Ibeu; Cecilia Mora Espejo, Universidad del Valle de México; Kate Nyhan, The New England School of English; Julie Oni, FLS; Willard Osman, The New England School of English; Olga Pagieva, ASA College; Manish Patel, FLS; Paige Poole, Universidad del Norte; Claudia Rebello, Ibeu; Lourdes Rey, Universidad del Norte; Michelle Reynolds, FLS International Boston Commons; Mary Ritter, NYU; Minerva Santos, Hostos; Sezer Sarioz, Saint Benoit PLS; Ebru Sinar, Tobb University; Beth Soll, NYU (Columbia); Christopher Stobart, Universidad del Norte; Guliz Uludag, Ufuk University; Debra Un, NYU; Hilal Unlusu, Saint Benoit PLS; María del Carmen Viruega Trejo, Universidad del Valle de México; Reda Vural, Atilim University; Douglas Waters, Universidad del Norte; Leyla Yucklik, Duzce University; Jorge Zepeda Porras, Universidad del Valle de México

A TEST OF
Endurance

1 FOCUS ON THE TOPIC

1. Look at the photo and read the title of the unit. Where is this man? What is this sport? What do you think this unit will be about?

2. *Endurance* is the ability to do something difficult or stressful over a long period of time. What kinds of sports require endurance?

3. Would you like to try an endurance sport yourself? Why or why not?

GO TO MyEnglishLab TO CHECK WHAT YOU KNOW.

VOCABULARY

1 🎧 Read and listen to the article about ultramarathons. Notice the boldfaced words.

EXTREME RUNNING
ULTRAMARATHONS

A **marathon** is a running race with a 26-mile **course**. An ultramarathon is a race longer than 26 miles, often 50 to 100 miles. There are two **formats** for ultramarathons: Some races have several short **stages** with breaks overnight. Other races go all day and night, with no stops until the runners finish.

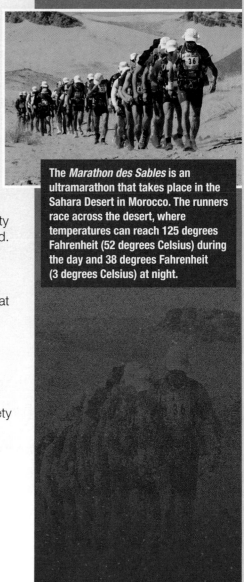

The *Marathon des Sables* is an ultramarathon that takes place in the Sahara Desert in Morocco. The runners race across the desert, where temperatures can reach 125 degrees Fahrenheit (52 degrees Celsius) during the day and 38 degrees Fahrenheit (3 degrees Celsius) at night.

The Racecourse

Ultramarathons take place all over the world, through many types of **terrain**. There are races through rainforests, from one city to another, over mountains and rivers, and across dry desert sand. Every ultramarathon is **unique** because each course is different.

Overnight

Many ultramarathons take several days to finish. Runners must eat and sleep on the course. In some races, food and supplies are carried in a car and the runners sleep in hotels. In other races, runners carry everything they need in backpacks, and they sleep outside in **tents**.

Running Safely

To stay healthy during an ultramarathon, runners must follow safety rules. For example, runners must drink their daily **ration** of water, even if they don't feel thirsty.

Crossing the Finish Line

What is in it for the runners?[1] Many runners say they **get into** ultramarathons because they feel that normal marathons are not challenging enough. They enjoy the **experience** of crossing the finish line and completing an extremely difficult event.

---

[1] **"What is in it for the runners?"** means "What are the advantages for the runners to run in the ultramarathons?"

2 Complete the definitions. Write the correct letter.

_g_   1. A **marathon** is _____.

_____   2. A **course** is _____.

_____   3. The **format** of something is _____.

_____   4. A **stage** is _____.

_____   5. **Terrain** is _____.

_____   6. Something that is **unique** is _____.

_____   7. A **tent** is _____.

_____   8. A **ration** is _____

_____   9. To **get into** something is _____.

_____   10. An **experience** is _____.

a. the only one of its kind

b. a piece of cloth supported by poles and rope that is used for sleeping outside

c. a specific amount of something that you are allowed to have

d. a step in a longer process

e. a type of land

f. to become interested in

g. ~~a 26-mile race~~

h. something that happens to you that affects the way you think or feel

i. the path of a race

j. the way its parts are arranged

▪▪▪ GO TO MyEnglishLab FOR MORE VOCABULARY PRACTICE.

PREVIEW

In this podcast, Jay Batchen talks about his experience as an ultramarathon runner.

🎧   Listen to an excerpt from the interview. Why do you think Jay runs in the marathon? Complete the sentence.

He runs in the marathon because _____.

MAIN IDEAS

1 🎧 Listen to the whole interview. Look again at your prediction from the Preview section. How did your prediction help you understand the interview?

2 All of the statements contain some FALSE information. Cross out the parts that are untrue and write corrections. Some statements can be corrected in more than one way.

        an endurance runner
1. Jay Batchen is ~~a sports reporter~~.

   or

     Tim
  ~~Jay Batchen~~ is a sports reporter.

2. Jay Batchen ran in the Marathon des Sables in 1999.

3. During the 1999 race, Jay married his wife, Lisa.

4. The Marathon des Sables has one stage.

5. Runners have to carry water with them.

6. Runners sleep outside under the stars.

7. Jay feels that the race was a terrible experience.

DETAILS

🎧 Listen again. Complete each statement. Circle the correct answer.

1. In 1999, Jay Batchen was _____ the race for a TV cable channel called the Discovery Channel.

   a. doing research about

   b. filming

   c. reporting on

2. Jay Batchen's future wife, Lisa, _____ the race in 1999.

   a. watched

   b. didn't finish

   c. won

3. The racecourse _____ every year, but it is always about 150 miles long.

    a. changes

    b. gets more difficult

    c. moves to a different country

4. The first three stages are all about _____.

    a. 10 miles long

    b. 20 miles long

    c. 26 miles long

5. The fourth stage is _____.

    a. 20 miles

    b. 50 miles

    c. a full marathon

6. The fifth stage is _____.

    a. 20 miles long

    b. 50 miles long

    c. a full marathon

7. Runners get _____ at checkpoints every few miles.

    a. a serving of food

    b. a ration of water

    c. medical help

8. Runners sleep in tents that are _____.

    a. small and light

    b. crowded and uncomfortable

    c. warm and quiet

(continued on next page)

9. Jay Batchen says that he experienced _____ during the race.

    a. heat, cold, and sandstorms

    b. hunger and thirst

    c. injuries to his feet

10. Jay Batchen calls the race a "life experience" because he _____.

    a. almost didn't finish the race

    b. shared the experience with other runners

    c. ran faster than the other runners

GO TO MyEnglishLab FOR MORE LISTENING PRACTICE.

MAKE INFERENCES

INFERRING MEANING FROM CONTEXT

An inference is a guess about something that is not directly stated. To make an inference, use information that you understand from what you hear.

A speaker may express an idea indirectly. The listener can infer the meaning based on the context. *Context* is the words that come just before and after a statement that help you understand its meaning.

Read and listen to the example. Notice the underlined information.

Example

JAY:	I filmed the event in 1999, which is actually the year my wife, Lisa Smith-Batchen, won the event. And that's how I ended up in Morocco and ended up learning about the event myself.
INTERVIEWER:	So did you know Lisa before that event, or you met her there?
JAY:	Met her there.
INTERVIEWER:	(laughing) OK, so you ended up marrying the winner of the race that you were filming.
JAY:	Yep.
INTERVIEWER:	Oh, very good.

When the interviewer laughs as he says, "OK, so you ended up marrying the winner of the race that you were filming," he is indirectly saying that Jay met his wife in an unusual way. The interviewer doesn't say these words directly. The listener has to infer the meaning.

1 🎧 Listen to the excerpts. Then read each question and choose the inferred meaning. Circle the correct answer.

Excerpt One

What does the interviewer mean when he says, "If you're able to stay standing at that point, I guess."?

a. Can you stand up by the end of the race?

b. You must be really tired by the end of the race.

c. I'm sure you want to stay standing after the race.

Excerpt Two

What does the interviewer mean when he says, "Well, you know, Jay, it doesn't sound like a whole lot of fun . . . "?

a. Most people say they didn't have fun.

b. I understand why you enjoyed the race.

c. It seems to me that it was a very difficult experience.

2 Work with a partner. Talk about the information that helped you find the answers.

EXPRESS OPINIONS

Work in a small group. Discuss the questions.

1. What's your opinion of Jay Batchen and the other runners in the Marathon des Sables? Do you admire them or do you think they are crazy? Explain.

2. What do you think is more important in an endurance race: physical strength or emotional strength? Or are they equally important? Explain.

■■■■■■■■■■■■■■■■■■■■■■■■■■■■■ GO TO MyEnglishLab TO GIVE YOUR OPINION ABOUT ANOTHER QUESTION.

VOCABULARY

1 Read the conversation. Notice the boldfaced words.

REPORTER: What **goal** do you hope to **achieve** in an ultramarathon?

RUNNER: I just do my best. It's hard to have the **motivation** to keep going. I know my **opponents** feel the same way, but we like the **challenge** of trying to do something really difficult.

2 Match the words with the definitions. Write the correct letter.

_____ **1.** goal   **a.** something that tests your skill or ability

_____ **2.** achieve   **b.** to succeed in getting a good result

_____ **3.** motivation   **c.** someone who tries to defeat you in a competition

_____ **4.** opponent   **d.** something you plan to do in the future

_____ **5.** challenge   **e.** the desire to do something

COMPREHENSION

1 🎧 Listen to an excerpt from a sports psychology class lecture about the motivation of endurance athletes. Complete each statement. Circle the correct answer.

1. Endurance athletes are often _____.

     a. very healthy

     b. high achievers

     c. professional athletes

2. They focus on achieving personal goals, not _____.

   a. finishing the event

   b. supporting other athletes

   c. winning the race

3. They choose goals that _____.

   a. are easy to achieve

   b. they have achieved before

   c. are a difficult challenge

4. They usually feel the other athletes are _____.

   a. friends who they can talk to

   b. opponents they want to beat

   c. partners in the experience

5. Endurance athletes are also motivated by _____.

   a. the strong emotions they feel while racing

   b. the prizes they win at the end of a race

   c. the exercise they get while racing

2 Work with a partner. Compare answers.

GO TO MyEnglishLab FOR MORE VOCABULARY PRACTICE.

LISTENING SKILL

1 🎧 Listen to an excerpt from the psychology lecture. What will the professor discuss next? What words does the speaker use to signal that information?

SIGNAL WORDS

Signal words tell the listener what to expect next. In a lecture, the speaker uses signal words to help the listener understand what the next idea will be.

🎧 Read and listen to the example. Notice the signal words.

Example

> PROFESSOR: Well, looking at the research, **there are a couple of points** that seem especially important.

The signal words tell the listener what to expect: The speaker will talk about two important points about an athlete's motivation for getting into extreme sports.

2 🎧 Listen to the excerpts. What signal words does the speaker use? Circle the correct answer.

1. To introduce point #1: the personality of endurance athletes

   a. *This first*

   b. *One of these*

   c. *The most important*

   d. *This one*

2. To introduce a contrast: focus on winning the race versus focus on personal goals

   a. *Otherwise*

   b. *However*

   c. *Sometimes*

   d. *Instead*

3. To introduce point #2: the relationship between athletes

   a. *Another*

   b. *The next*

   c. *One more*

   d. *Finally*

4. To introduce a result: the effects of the emotional high

    a. *As a result*

    b. *Because of this*

    c. *Consequently*

    d. *So*

GO TO MyEnglishLab FOR MORE SKILL PRACTICE.

CONNECT THE LISTENINGS

STEP 1: Organize

🎧 Listen to an excerpt from Listening One and read the excerpts from Listening Two. Then write examples from Listening One that support the ideas in Listening Two.

LISTENING ONE: Ultrarunner Jay Batchen	LISTENING TWO: Sports Psychology
1. What are some of the challenges that Jay Batchen faced?	"As a group these people tend to be high achievers. . . . They like difficult challenges and they aren't happy with goals that are easy to achieve."
2. What are Jay Batchen's personal goals?	"And when setting goals, most endurance athletes don't focus on winning the race. Instead, they have personal goals, like maybe just finishing the race is enough, or finishing with a better time than before."
3. How does Jay Batchen feel about the other athletes in his race?	"In general, endurance athletes don't see the other athletes in a race as opponents or people they're trying to beat. Instead, they see them as partners—partners in this unique adventure, doing something that no one else is doing."

STEP 2: Synthesize

Work with a partner. Do you think the professor of sports psychology would agree with the statements? Discuss your answers. Use examples from Step 1: Organize to support your opinion.

    1. Running in the Marathon des Sables was a difficult challenge for Jay Batchen.

    2. Jay Batchen was motivated by his relationship with other athletes during the race.

    3. Jay Batchen was motivated by the personal goal of winning the race.

GO TO MyEnglishLab TO CHECK WHAT YOU LEARNED.

VOCABULARY

REVIEW

Read the clues and complete the crossword puzzle. Use vocabulary from Listenings One and Two.

Across

2. My _____ is to compete in three races this year, but I don't know if I'll have time.

6. In the Polar Circle Run, the _____ is steep and covered with ice.

8. The New York City _____ is the largest running race in the world.

10. Jay Batchen had an important life _____ running in the Marathon des Sables.

12. I tried to beat my _____, but he was faster and won the race.

13. The race _____ is the same length every year.

14. Many athletes _____ _____ endurance sports because they want a challenge.

Down

1. The runners enjoyed the _____ of doing something difficult.

3. We finished the first _____ of the race today, and the second one is tomorrow.

4. This is a _____ race. No other race is like it.

5. My _____ for doing sports is to stay healthy and have fun.

7. I hope to _____ my dream of running in the Olympics.

9. I don't want to drink my _____ of water now because I might be thirsty later.

11. The Super Mountain Race has a two-day _____ with an overnight run.

1 Read the conversation between a reporter and an ultra-long-distance swimmer. Notice the boldfaced words.

REPORTER: How did it go out there?

SWIMMER: I'm OK, but it was a tough day. I fell behind the group about halfway, and that really **(1) threw me for a loop**. I never felt the same after that.

REPORTER: How come?

SWIMMER: Well, sometimes I can **(2) be my own worst enemy**. I mean, I start thinking negative thoughts, and I don't swim well.

REPORTER: How did you keep yourself going after that?

SWIMMER: I **(3) set my heart on** finishing the race. I really want it. I got a good start, and I don't want to **(4) blow my chance**.

REPORTER: So, after your problems today, what's your plan for tomorrow?

SWIMMER: Well, I want to enjoy myself more.

REPORTER: **(5) Easier said than done!**

SWIMMER: So true! But I know **(6) I have what it takes** to finish the race, so I just need to go out and try my best.

2 Match the boldfaced words with their meanings. Write the correct number.

_____ **a.** decided that I really wanted to do this

_____ **b.** miss my opportunity by making a mistake

_____ **c.** I have the ability to be successful.

_____ **d.** surprised and confused me

_____ **e.** behave in a way that causes problems later

_____ **f.** That's really difficult to do.

3 Work with a partner. Practice the conversation in Exercise 1.

CREATE

Work with a partner. Think about an important goal you have in your life. It can be a goal in sports, school, work, or other areas. Take turns asking and answering the questions. Use the words and phrases from the box in your answers.

Questions

1. What is your goal?

2. When did you set this goal?

3. What is your motivation for setting this goal?

3. How is your experience so far?

4. What challenges make it difficult to achieve your goal?

5. Do you have what it takes? Why or why not?

be my own worst enemy	motivation
blow my chance	opponent
easier said than done	set (your) heart on
endurance	throw (me) for a loop
format	unique

Example

STUDENT A: What is your goal?

STUDENT B: My goal is to be a newspaper reporter.

STUDENT A: When did you set this goal?

STUDENT B: I set my heart on it in high school when I worked on the school newspaper. I really enjoyed the challenge.

GO TO MyEnglishLab FOR MORE VOCABULARY PRACTICE.

GRAMMAR

1 Read the excerpt from an article about motivation. The boldfaced words are reflexive and reciprocal pronouns. Draw an arrow from the pronouns to the words they refer to.

What motivates an extreme athlete like Jay Batchen to push **himself** to the limit? One thing we know is that athletes like Jay tend to be risk takers. They feel excited when they put **themselves** in risky or dangerous situations. This feeling can become stronger when athletes compete against **one another**. For example, if an extreme skier sees another skier doing a difficult jump, she might challenge **herself** to do an even more dangerous jump.

REFLEXIVE AND RECIPROCAL PRONOUNS

1. Use a **reflexive pronoun** when the subject and object of a sentence are the same person or thing. The reflexive pronouns are: *myself* *ourselves* *yourself* *yourselves* *herself* *himself* *themselves* *itself*	*Jay Batchen pushes **himself** to the limit.* *They put **themselves** in dangerous situations.*
2. Use *yourself / yourselves* in **imperative sentences** that are reflexive. Use: • *yourself* when the subject is singular • *yourselves* when the subject is plural NOTE: In imperative sentences, the subject is *you*, even though it isn't stated.	*(you) Believe in **yourself** and you will succeed.* *(you) Prepare **yourselves** for a tough race.*
3. Use a **reciprocal pronoun** when the subject and object are the same people, and the people have a relationship. Use: • *each other* for two people. • *one another* for more than two people. NOTE: Often people use *each other* and *one another* in the same way.	*Marge and Susan competed against **each other**.* *The athletes competed against **one another**.*

(continued on next page)

A Test of Endurance   17

4. Reciprocal pronouns and plural reflexive pronouns have different meanings.	*Marge and Susan helped **each other**.* (Marge helped Susan, and Susan helped Marge.) *Marge and Susan helped **themselves**.* (Marge helped herself, and Susan helped herself.)

2 Complete the conversation with the correct reflexive and reciprocal pronouns.

PIERRE: This is Pierre Blanc, reporting on the Extreme Alpine Road Race in France. I'm talking to Tomas Bergetti, coach of cyclist Bridgit Jacobsen. Tomas, what does Bridgit do to prepare

(1) _____ for this race?

TOMAS: Well, she pushes (2) _____ pretty hard. She gets up at 4:00 A.M. every day to ride, and she only takes one day off a month!

PIERRE: Wow! I know her brother Hans is on the same team. Do Bridgit and Hans help

(3) _____ with training?

TOMAS: Absolutely! And they're both part of a bigger team. All the athletes help

(4) _____ to set personal goals.

PIERRE: You must be very proud of her big win in the race today!

TOMAS: Yes, the whole team is very happy. We're all going to reward

(5) _____ with a big dinner!

PIERRE: That's great! One last question. What do you do to motivate Bridgit to keep going?

TOMAS: I always say, "Believe in (6) _____!" You have to have confidence if you want to win.

3 Work with a partner. Imagine what Bridgit and her teammates do in these situations. Choose verbs from the box and use reflexive and reciprocal pronouns in your answers. Think of more than one answer for each situation.

be disappointed in	compete against	feel sorry for	push
blame	enjoy	imagine	support
challenge	feel proud of	make / force	tell

Example

A: What does Bridgit do if she starts feeling tired at the end of a race?

B: She imagines herself crossing the finish line.

What does Bridgit do if . . .

1. she starts feeling tired at the end of a race?

2. she sleeps late and misses her morning training?

3. she goes to a party to celebrate winning a race?

4. she doesn't achieve her training goals?

5. her teammate wins a race?

What do Bridgit and her teammates do / feel . . .

6. when they are racing together?

7. if their team wins?

8. if their team loses?

GO TO MyEnglishLab FOR MORE GRAMMAR PRACTICE.

PRONUNCIATION

EXPRESSIONS WITH *OTHER*

The word *other* joins very closely to the word in front of it or the word that follows it. In **another**, the two words (*an* and *other*) are written together. In the expression **each other**, the two words are written separately, but they are joined just as closely together.

🎧 Read and listen to the conversation. Notice the boldfaced words.

Example

A: **The other** night I was talking to my roommate about starting a regular exercise program. She wants to start, too.

B: You should do it together. You'll motivate **each other**.

A: I have **another** motivation—the clothes in my closet that don't fit anymore!

1. Join *other* to the word before it. Pronounce the two words as if they were one word. Say "eachother."

2. Pronounce the "th" in *other* with the tip of your tongue between your teeth. Try it.

3. When *the* precedes *other*, it is pronounced /thē/ (the *e* sounds like the vowel in *tree*). Use *the* pronounced /thē/ to join to *other*. Try it: /thē/ *other*

1 🎧 Listen to the phrases and repeat them. Then choose three phrases and say them to the class. Join the words together closely and don't forget to pronounce **th** (/ð/) correctly.

1. the other night (recently, at night)

2. the other day (recently)

3. something or other (an idiom for "something")

4. one another

5. each other

6. some other

7. one thing or another

8. every other day (on alternate days: Monday, Wednesday, Friday, etc.)

2 Fill in the blanks with expressions from Exercise 1. Check your answers with a partner's and then practice reading the sentences to your partner. Join words together and pronounce the "**th**" in "**other**" carefully.

1. _____ _____ _____ my two roommates and I go for a long walk.

2. _____ _____ _____ we were walking in the park behind a very old couple.

3. They were holding hands and talking to _____ _____.

4. The woman slipped on _____ _____ _____ and fell.

5. _____ _____ people were passing by, but they didn't do anything.

6. We ran to help them, and when we saw them, we realized we all knew _____ _____. They live in our building.

3 Work with a partner. Create five short conversations by matching Student A's part with Student B's part. Then practice the conversations. The underlined words are idioms with "**other**." Do you know what they mean?

Student A

1. Sharon's sons are <u>at each other's throats</u> all the time. She doesn't know what to do.

2. This has been one of the worst days of my life.

3. What's the difference between a rainproof tent and a rain-resistant tent?

4. The lecture was really hard. I don't think I remember anything the professor said.

5. The elderly couple that I helped in the park last week brought me a cake.

Student B

a. Nothing, as far as I'm concerned—<u>six of one, half a dozen of another</u>.

b. Me neither—the material went <u>in one ear and out the other</u>.

c. I guess it's true that <u>one good turn deserves another</u>.

d. She might not be able to do anything. My brother and I fought with each other until he went away to school.

e. Don't give up. <u>Tomorrow's another day</u>.

SPEAKING SKILL

ASKING FOR AND EXPRESSING OPINIONS

To keep a conversation going (and to make it interesting), it is important for everyone to share ideas. To do this, express your opinion, ask for other people's opinions, and agree or disagree with other people's opinions.

🎧 Read and listen to the conversation. Notice the language used to ask for and express opinions.

Example

SUNG LEE: Look at that guy. **What do you think** he's doing?

AHMED: **It looks like** he's running forward and then backward. Maybe he's training for a race.

ELI: **I'm not sure**. See how slowly he's going? He can't be a racer.

AHMED: **You're right**. He is pretty slow. **I think** he's probably just doing that for fun.

To Ask for an Opinion	
Use *What do you think (about)* . . . ? to ask for a general opinion.	*What do you think about extreme sports?*
Use *Do you think (that . . .)* / *Do you agree (with)* . . . ? to ask about specific points.	*Do you think extreme sports are dangerous?*
	Do you agree (with Eli) that extreme sports are dangerous?

To Express an Opinion	
Use *I think* to sound stronger and more certain.	*I think Bridgit won the race.*
Use *I'm pretty sure* or *It seems like* to sound less certain and / or more polite.	*I'm pretty sure Bridgit won the race.*
	It seems like Bridgit won the race.

To Agree	
To agree with someone use:	
I think . . .	*I think Ron is the best runner.*
Yeah / Yes. . . . (I think) You're right.	*Yeah, he is. I think you're right.*
I agree (with name).	*I agree (with Michelle).*

To Disagree

To disagree with someone use:

Indirect:

I don't know.

I'm not sure about that.

Direct:

I don't think so.

I disagree *(with name).*

I don't know. *Jack is a great runner, too.*

I'm not sure about that. *Jack is a great runner, too.*

I don't think so. *Jack is better.*

I disagree *(with Kyoko). Jack is better.*

Indirect disagreement sounds more polite.

Direct disagreement sounds stronger and can be less polite.

---

1 Work with a partner. Read both conversations and discuss the differences. Which conversation is more direct? Which is more indirect and polite? Underline the words and phrases that helped you decide.

Conversation 1

A: I think extreme sports are the most dangerous sports.

B: I don't think so. All sports can be dangerous.

C: You're right. I think that athletes hurt themselves in all sports, not just extreme sports.

Conversation 2

A: I think that extreme sports are the most dangerous sports.

B: I'm not sure about that. It seems to me that all sports can be dangerous.

C: Yeah. I'm pretty sure that athletes hurt themselves in all sports, not just extreme sports.

2 Work in a group of three. Look at the pictures of the athletes. Discuss how each athlete is feeling. Make sure that everyone in the group gets to express an opinion. Under each picture write the adjective(s) that you think best describe(s) the athlete's feelings.

Example

ROBERTO: In Picture A, I think the guy on the left is angry. Look at his face. Doesn't he look angry?

KEIKO: I don't know. See how he's looking at the ball? It seems like he's trying to get it. What do you think, Maria?

MARIA: I agree with Roberto. He looks angry to me.

A

angry

B

_____

C

_____

D

_____

GO TO MyEnglishLab FOR MORE SKILL PRACTICE AND TO CHECK WHAT YOU LEARNED.

FINAL SPEAKING TASK

An **aphorism** is a short, wise expression that is easy to remember. It expresses an idea or belief in a new and interesting way.

In this activity, you will discuss aphorisms about motivation, write one of your own, and explain its meaning.

Work in a small group. Follow the steps. Try to use the vocabulary, grammar, pronunciation, and listening and speaking skills that you learned in the unit.*

STEP 1: Read and discuss the aphorisms in the box, Quotes on Motivation.

- What are the athletes saying about their motivation for running? Explain.
- Which aphorism do you like best? Why?
- Which aphorism expresses an idea or feeling you have had? Explain.

STEP 2: As a group, create an aphorism about motivation. Think of a situation in which a person needs motivation, such as playing sports, studying, working, practicing a musical instrument, or anything else. Give your opinion of the different ideas until the group agrees on an expression.

STEP 3: Write the aphorism on the board or on a big piece of paper. As a group, share the aphorism with the class and explain its meaning.

Quotes on Motivation

1. "Motivation is what gets you started. Habit is what keeps you going."
   —Jim Ryun

2. "When I run a long race, I get to meet some new people—including myself."
   —Anonymous

3. "The fear of not finishing is often greater than the fear of pain."
   —Laurie Dexter

4. "The heart controls the mind, and the mind controls the body."
   —Jim Lampley

5. "Find the joy in the journey—the finish line will come soon enough."
   —Anonymous

6. "The glory of sport comes from dedication, determination, and desire."
   — Jackie Joyner-Kersee

---

*For Alternative Speaking Topics, see page 27.

Listen to the explanations of the aphorisms. Ask questions if you don't understand something. Which aphorism did you like best? Discuss your choice with your group.

UNIT PROJECT

STEP 1: Choose an extreme sport from the box or think of your own.

bungee jumping	extreme skiing	ironman triathlon
cave diving	free-diving	kite boarding
class 5 river rafting	hang gliding	parasailing
cliff diving	ice climbing	rappelling
deep-sea diving	Iditarod	sky diving

STEP 2: Research the sport on the Internet or in the library. Find a picture of the sport and answer the questions.

1. What do you do in this sport?

2. What is dangerous about this sport?

3. Why do people like this sport?

4. What other information can you find about this sport?

STEP 3: Present your picture and information to the class.

ALTERNATIVE SPEAKING TOPICS

Discuss one of the topics. Use the vocabulary and grammar from the unit.

1. In Listening Two, the professor talks about two motivations for endurance sports: the satisfaction of achieving goals and the closeness to other athletes. Can you think of other reasons that extreme athletes compete in their sports?

2. Research has shown that a large number of emergency room doctors take part in extreme sports. What do you think the reason is? Can you think of other professions that might require the personality of the extreme athlete?

GO TO MyEnglishLab TO DISCUSS ONE OF THE ALTERNATIVE TOPICS, WATCH A VIDEO ABOUT A PROFESSIONAL BMX BIKER, AND TAKE THE UNIT I ACHIEVEMENT TEST.

AVOIDING IDENTITY Theft

1 FOCUS ON THE TOPIC

1. Identity theft happens when thieves steal personal information. Look at the photo. What items in the wallet could the thief use for identity theft?

2. Identity theft is the fastest-growing crime around the world. Thieves steal more than $200 billion from victims each year. Why do you think this crime is increasing?

3. How can you keep your personal information safe?

GO TO MyEnglishLab TO CHECK WHAT YOU KNOW.

LISTENING ONE **LILY'S STORY**

VOCABULARY

1 🎧 Thieves can use the Internet in many ways to steal people's identities. Read and listen to the article about "phishing." Notice the boldfaced words.

Identity Theft Online:
Phishing

A few months ago, Henry Park received an e-mail message from his bank. The message said there was a problem with his account. It said to follow a link[1] to the bank's web site. He went to a web page that asked him to **confirm** the information about his bank account by entering his bank card number and password. "I followed the instructions and got a message that everything was fine, so I forgot about it," Mr. Park said.

A few weeks later, Mr. Park received a credit card bill for almost $10,000. There were **charges** from a department store[2] for a flat screen TV and a diamond ring. However, Mr. Park hadn't made any of these **purchases** and had never **authorized** anyone to use his credit card.

Mr. Park immediately called the bank to **file a complaint**. Then he found out that he was the **victim** of the fastest-growing type of online fraud:[3] phishing (pronounced "fishing").

How does phishing work?
Criminals pretend to work for real companies. They send e-mail messages to thousands of people. They trick people into going to a fraudulent web site (which looks like a real site) and giving out their personal information. Then the thieves use the information to commit identity theft. In Mr. Park's case, the thief used the information to open a credit card in Mr. Park's name.

The experience has made Mr. Park more aware of the dangers of phishing. "I feel **exposed** now, like someone will do this to me again. And I'm more **paranoid**. I don't trust e-mail anymore."

Keep yourself safe from phishing
- Be careful about e-mail messages and websites that ask for personal information. Don't give out information that a thief could use as **proof of identification**, such as a driver's license or passport number.
- If you think you have been a victim of phishing, **deal with** it right away by calling your bank and the police. Don't wait until you start getting bills.

---

[1]**link:** a highlighted word or phrase on an Internet web page or in an e-mail message that takes you to another web page

[2]**department store:** a large store that sells many different kinds of products

[3]**fraud:** the crime of misleading people in order to get money or goods

2 Match the words with the definitions. Write the correct letter.

_____ **1.** confirm

_____ **2.** charge

_____ **3.** purchase

_____ **4.** authorize

_____ **5.** file a complaint

_____ **6.** victim

_____ **7.** exposed

_____ **8.** paranoid

_____ **9.** proof of identification

_____ **10.** deal with

a. believing that you cannot trust other people

b. the amount on a bill that you have to pay for something

c. in danger of being harmed

d. to say or prove that something is true

e. something that has been bought

f. documents, or papers, that show who you are

g. to do what is necessary to solve a problem

h. to give permission for something

i. someone who has been hurt by someone or something

j. to send a letter saying that something bad or illegal happened

GO TO MyEnglishLab FOR MORE VOCABULARY PRACTICE.

PREVIEW

Lily's wallet was stolen at a restaurant. The thief used her personal information to open credit cards in her name. In this story, Lily describes what happened next.

🎧 Listen to the excerpt from Lily's story. Circle the correct answer. Discuss your answer with the class.

This is an excerpt from _____ of the story.

    a. the beginning

    b. the middle

    c. the end

MAIN IDEAS

1 🎧 Listen to the whole story. Look again at your prediction from the Preview section. How did your prediction help you understand the story?

2 Circle the correct answer. Compare answers with a classmate.

1. How did Lily find out that her identity had been stolen?

    a. A store called her.

    b. She got a bill in the mail.

    c. The police came to her house.

2. What happened after Lily found out about the identity theft?

    a. She got bills for purchases that she didn't make.

    b. She got phone calls from a lot of different stores.

    c. She got a letter from the police.

3. How did Lily deal with the bills she received?

    a. She went to the stores and complained to the manager.

    b. She wrote letters to the stores and explained what happened.

    c. She sent the bills back to the stores without paying them.

4. How did being a victim of identity theft affect Lily?

    a. She had to borrow money to pay the bills.

    b. She doesn't use credit cards anymore.

    c. She worries that it will happen again.

DETAILS

Listen again. Complete the summary of Lily's story. Circle the correct words.

Lily got a phone call from a **(1) jewelry / department** store saying that someone with her name had purchased a **(2) computer / diamond ring**. They wanted her to authorize the purchase. Lily knew there was something wrong because she was at **(3) home / work** all day. The woman on the phone said that Lily was probably a victim of identity theft. She told Lily to **(4) file a complaint / go to the police station**.

In the next week, Lily received almost **(5) four / forty** bills from different stores, totaling about **(6) $13,000 / $30,000** in charges. She felt exposed because the thief knew her **(7) name and address / bank account number**. She didn't know what to do.

To deal with the problem, she sent **(8) the police report / her proof of identification** to all the stores and confirmed that she had not made the purchases. She stopped getting new bills after about **(9) four / eight** months.

Lily worries about becoming a victim again. She thinks that **(10) getting a credit card is too easy / paying off a credit card bill is difficult** at most department stores. She thinks everyone should be worried about identity theft.

GO TO MyEnglishLab FOR MORE LISTENING PRACTICE.

MAKE INFERENCES

A speaker may use *intonation* to express his or her feelings indirectly. The listener can infer the speaker's emotion by paying attention to intonation.

🎧 Read and listen to the examples. What is Speaker B feeling in each example? Notice how the intonation changes how the speaker feels.

Example 1

A: What did the thief steal from you?

B: Five thousand dollars. A diamond ring.

Example 2

A: Somebody who has your name has purchased a diamond ring for $5,000.

B: Five thousand dollars! A diamond ring!

In Example 1, the statement has falling intonation. Speaker B is not expressing emotion. She is reporting that a ring was stolen.

In Example 2, the statement has rising-falling intonation. Speaker B is expressing surprise about the purchase of a ring.

1 🎧 Listen to the pairs of statements. Identify the feeling based on the intonation. Is the speaker reporting information or is the speaker surprised? Write "<u>A</u>" or "<u>B</u>" in the blank.

1. "I'm going to get a bill for this."

   Reporting: Statement _____

   Surprised: Statement _____

2. "We have a problem."

   Reporting: Statement _____

   Surprised: Statement _____

3. "You don't need proof of identification."

   Reporting: Statement _____

   Surprised: Statement _____

2 Work with a partner. Talk about the information that helped you find the answers.

EXPRESS OPINIONS

Work with a partner. Discuss the statements. Give reasons for your opinion. Then work with a different partner and have a new discussion.

1. I feel more paranoid about identity theft after hearing Lily's story.

2. We should try not to carry much personal information in our wallets.

3. There is really nothing we can do to prevent identity theft.

4. Customers don't want to wait while stores check their identity.

▪▪▪▪▪▪▪▪▪▪▪▪▪▪▪▪▪▪▪▪▪▪▪▪▪▪▪▪ *GO TO* MyEnglishLab *TO GIVE YOUR OPINION ABOUT ANOTHER QUESTION.*

LISTENING TWO PUBLIC SERVICE ANNOUNCEMENTS

VOCABULARY

1 Read the message from a public service announcement (PSA[1]). Notice the boldfaced words.

With only a few pieces of information, it's easy for a thief to **(a) commit** identity theft. Fortunately, there are ways to **(b) protect** yourself and reduce the **(c) risk** of becoming a victim. One helpful **(d) tip** is to **(e) shred** important documents before you throw them away.

2 Match the boldfaced words from the message with the definitions. Write the correct letter.

_____ 1. a helpful piece of advice

_____ 2. the possibility that something bad may happen

_____ 3. to do something illegal

_____ 4. to keep someone or yourself safe from harm

_____ 5. to cut something into small pieces

---

[1] **PSA:** PSAs are short presentations that give people helpful information. You often hear them on the radio or on TV.

COMPREHENSION

🎧 Listen to two PSAs about how to protect yourself from identity theft. Check (✓) the tips that you hear.

- [ ] **1.** Get a locked mailbox.

- [ ] **2.** Be careful about giving out personal information.

- [ ] **3.** Check your bank and credit card statements every month.

- [ ] **4.** Shred important papers before throwing them away.

- [ ] **5.** Leave your identification at home if you don't need it.

GO TO MyEnglishLab *FOR MORE VOCABULARY PRACTICE.*

LISTENING SKILL

1 🎧 Listen to an excerpt from PSA 1. What question does the announcer ask? What is the answer? Why do you think the speaker asks a question?

RHETORICAL QUESTIONS

Rhetorical questions are used to direct the listener's attention. The speaker doesn't expect an answer from the listener. Instead, a rhetorical question makes the listener pay attention to an important idea.

🎧 Read and listen to the example. Notice the rhetorical question.

Example

ANNOUNCER: **Think you're safe from identity theft?** Think again.

The rhetorical question directs the listener to the idea: *Don't think you are safe from identity theft.*

NOTE: The speaker uses a shortened, informal form of the question "Do you think you're safe . . . ?"

2 🎧 Listen to PSA 2. The speaker asks two rhetorical questions. What does the speaker want us to pay attention to? Write the important ideas.

1. "Hear that sound? That's the sound of a crime being committed."

    Important idea: _____

    _____

2. "Hear that sound? That's the sound of someone protecting himself from becoming a victim of identity theft."

    Important idea: _____

    _____

■■■ GO TO MyEnglishLab FOR MORE SKILL PRACTICE.

CONNECT THE LISTENINGS

STEP 1: Organize

🎧 Listen to Listening One and Listening Two (PSA 1 only) again. Then complete the chart with the details about identity theft.

	LISTENING ONE: Lily's Story	LISTENING TWO: PSA 1
1. How do thieves steal personal information?	• by _____ _____ • by taking information from receipts	• by stealing your mail • by _____ _____ • by _____ _____
2. How can people prevent identity theft?	• by ripping up receipts • by _____ _____	• by _____ _____ • by _____ _____ • by shredding documents before throwing them away

Work with a partner. One person is a victim of identity theft. The other person is a security expert. Complete the conversation using information from Step 1: Organize. Switch roles and repeat the conversation.

VICTIM: I don't understand how this happened. How do thieves steal personal information?

SECURITY EXPERT: Well, there are many ways. For example, _____

_____
Give examples.

_____.

So, what do you do now to keep your personal information safe?

VICTIM: Hmm, well I, _____.

_____
Give examples.

_____.

SECURITY EXPERT: That's good, but it's not enough. _____?

_____.
Ask a rhetorical question.

_____
Give advice.

_____.

GO TO MyEnglishLab TO CHECK WHAT YOU LEARNED.

VOCABULARY

A word can have a meaning that is positive (good), negative (bad), or neutral (neither good nor bad). This is called the **connotation** of a word or expression. For example:

POSITIVE	NEGATIVE	NEUTRAL
safe	fraud	department store

1   Work with a partner. Complete the chart with the words from the box.

authorize	exposed	purchase
charge	file a complaint	risk
commit	paranoid	shred
confirm	proof of identification	tip
deal with	protect	victim

2   Compare your chart with another pair's chart. Discuss the reasons for your choices.

1 Read the e-mails from Lucia to her friend Shu Li. Notice the boldfaced words.

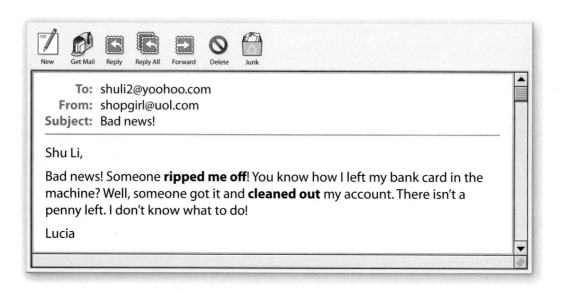

To: shuli2@yoohoo.com
From: shopgirl@uol.com
Subject: Bad news!

Shu Li,

Bad news! Someone **ripped me off**! You know how I left my bank card in the machine? Well, someone got it and **cleaned out** my account. There isn't a penny left. I don't know what to do!

Lucia

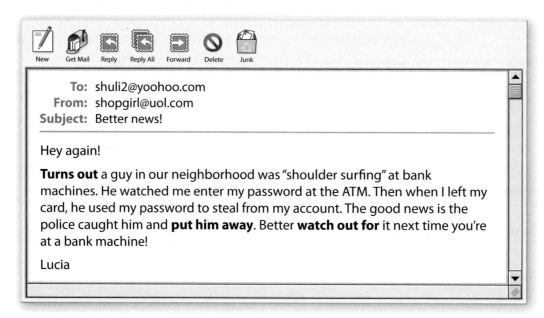

To: shuli2@yoohoo.com
From: shopgirl@uol.com
Subject: Better news!

Hey again!

Turns out a guy in our neighborhood was "shoulder surfing" at bank machines. He watched me enter my password at the ATM. Then when I left my card, he used my password to steal from my account. The good news is the police caught him and **put him away**. Better **watch out for** it next time you're at a bank machine!

Lucia

2 Circle the best synonym or definition for each boldfaced word.

1. **rip off**   steal   keep

2. **clean out**   steal everything   pay

3. **turn out**   cause   result

4. **put away**   let out of jail   put in jail

5. **watch out for**   ignore   be careful of

CREATE

Work in groups of three. Play the game To Tell the Truth. Follow the steps.

Game: To Tell the Truth

1. Think of a time when something was stolen from you. Form a group with two other students and share your story.

2. One member of your group will tell his or her *true* story to the class. The other two members will each tell a story that is not true. Decide who will tell the truth and who will lie. Each group member writes down five words or phrases from the vocabulary box to use in his or her story.

3. Present your stories to the class (Remember: One story is true, the other two are false. Each story contains five words from the vocabulary box.) After each story, take questions from the class. At the end, ask the class to guess which story is true.

4. Return to your seat to listen to another group's stories.

authorize	file a complaint	risk
charge	paranoid	shred
clean out	proof of identification	tip
commit	protect	turn out
confirm	purchase	victim
deal with	put away	watch out for
exposed	rip off	

GO TO MyEnglishLab *FOR MORE VOCABULARY PRACTICE.*

GRAMMAR

1 Look at the picture and read the conversation. Notice the boldfaced **modals of advice**.

DAUGHTER: I got my first credit card in the mail today!

MOTHER: You **should** sign it right away! And you**'d better not** lose it.

DAUGHTER: Mom, you **ought to** stop worrying so much!

MODALS OF ADVICE

1. Use **should** to ask for advice.	***Should** I show them proof of identification?* *What **should** I do if someone steals my passport?*
2. Use **should**, **should not**, and **ought to** to give advice. NOTE: **Ought to** is generally not used with a negative in American English.	*He **should** get a locked mailbox.* *They **shouldn't** send personal information by e-mail.* *You **ought to** ask your boss to keep your personal information in a locked file.*
3. Use **had better ('d better)** and **had better not ('d better not)** to give strong advice.	*We**'d better** shred those papers.* *You**'d better not** throw those papers in the trash.*

2 Complete the sentence. Circle the correct answer.

1. Nasir wants to throw away some old bank statements. He _____ shred them.

  a. should   **b.** ought   **c.** better

2. Mira's mail was stolen. She _____ better buy a locked mailbox.

  a. should   **b.** ought   **c.** had

3. Someone called Azim and asked for a donation. He _____ give out his credit card number over the phone.

  a. should   **b.** shouldn't   **c.** better not

4. Lily got a bill for charges she didn't make. She _____ to file a complaint.

    a. ought   **b.** should   **c.** had better

5. Misako got an e-mail asking for her credit card account number. She _____ not send the information.

    a. shouldn't   **b.** had better   **c.** ought

6. Chong Li gets money from a bank machine. He _____ make sure nobody is watching him.

    a. should   **b.** ought not   **c.** ought

7. The clerk asked Nicola to write her driver's license number on a check. She _____ not do that.

    a. better   **b.** should   **c.** ought to

8. Abraham got a passport. He _____ lose it.

    a. ought   **b.** should   **c.** had better not

3 Work in a group of three. Take turns asking for and giving advice.

Example

STUDENT A: I haven't received any mail for three days. What **should** I do?

STUDENT B: You **should** check with the post office to see whether someone is stealing your mail.

STUDENT C: If someone is stealing your mail, you **ought to** contact the police.

1. I saw someone take a letter out of my neighbor's mailbox.

2. I get phone calls every day from a man I don't know. He's trying to sell me magazines.

3. Someone took some files from my office. They had personal information in them.

4. I usually have five credit cards in my wallet, but right now I seem to be missing one.

5. I have to mail my passport to New York to get a visa.

6. An online store sent me an e-mail asking for my credit card number.

PRONUNCIATION

RECOGNIZING COMPOUNDS

Compounds are two nouns used together to name one thing, for example, *mailbox*. In *mailbox* the two nouns are written together as one word. These compounds are easy to recognize. Other compounds, like *identity theft* and *credit card*, are written as two words. Compounds have a special pattern of stress and pitch.

🎧 Read and listen to the compounds. Repeat them.

Examples

1. *post office*
2. *credit card*
3. *identity theft*
4. *garbage can*
5. *mailbox*
6. *police station*
7. *bank account*
8. *roommate*

The first word has the heaviest stress and higher pitch. The second word is not stressed as much and has lower pitch: ***post*** *office* / ***credit*** *card*

Sometimes another noun follows a compound, making a three-word compound: *identity theft victim*. The first word has the heaviest stress and highest pitch. The following words have less stress and lower pitch: ***identity*** *theft victim*

1 🎧 Listen to the nouns and repeat them. Circle the words that are pronounced as compounds, with heavy stress and high pitch on the first word. Compare your answers with a partner's.

1. diamond ring
2. charge accounts
3. online
4. e-mail
5. Internet fraud
6. police report
7. five thousand dollars
8. ID
9. web site
10. personal information
11. 10-dollar bill
12. mailbox key

2 Work with a partner. Answer the questions. Pronounce the compounds correctly.

1. What's in your wallet?

2. What should you do if you lose your wallet or if someone steals it? Has this ever happened to you? What did you do?

SPEAKING SKILL

KEEPING A CONVERSATION GOING

To keep a conversation going, both speakers need to *show that they are listening* and sometimes *encourage the other person to keep talking.*

🎧 Listen to and read the conversation. Notice the underlined words and the rising or falling intonation for each.

Example

A: So, I got a call from this guy . . .

B: Uh-huh.

A: And he wanted me to give money to some organization called Amazon Rainforest something or other. You know what I'm talking about?

B: Yes. Go on.

A: Anyway, I got this weird feeling from him. Basically, I didn't trust him.

B: So, what did you do?

A: Well, I just hung up on him. You'd better be careful about these things, right?

B: Right.

TO SHOW YOU ARE LISTENING	TO ENCOURAGE THE SPEAKER TO KEEP TALKING
Yeah . . . (rising)	*Yes. Go on.* (falling)
Uh-huh . . . (rising)	*And?* (rising)
OK . . . (rising)	*So?* (rising)
Right. (falling)	*And then what?* (falling)
Wow! (falling)	*So what did he / she say / did you do / happened next?* (falling)

Work with a partner. Complete the conversations. Choose language to show you are listening or to encourage the speaker. Then practice reading the conversations out loud with your partner. Switch roles and repeat.

Conversation 1

A: So, I was in my apartment and saw this man outside looking through my garbage.

B: _____

A: Well, at first I thought it was someone from our building, but then I realized I didn't recognize him.

B: _____

(continued on next page)

A: So, I asked my roommate to go outside with me. Better not to go alone, right?

B: _____

A: So, we went up to the guy, and I said, "Are you looking for something?"

B: _____

A: And he got really scared, dropped some papers he was holding, and ran. So I quickly grabbed the papers . . .

B: _____

A: And they were my bank statements.

Conversation 2

A: Remember that apartment I tried to rent?

B: _____

A: Well, the owner tried to rip me off. He took information from my application form and opened a credit card in my name!

B: _____ How did you find out?

A: I started getting all these bills for charges on an account that I didn't open.

B: _____

A: And then I remembered John Day was the last person I'd given my personal information to.

B: _____

A: Well, I found out that he's done this before. Two years ago he was caught and put away for identity theft.

▪▪▪▪▪▪▪▪▪▪▪▪▪▪▪▪▪▪▪▪▪▪▪▪▪ GO TO MyEnglishLab FOR MORE SKILL PRACTICE AND TO CHECK WHAT YOU LEARNED.

FINAL SPEAKING TASK

A role play is a short performance. The actors take on roles, or become characters, and act out a situation. Often the situations are similar to experiences that people might have in real life.

In this activity, you will create and perform a 3–5-minute role play about identity theft.

Work in a group of three. Follow the steps. Try to use the vocabulary, grammar, pronunciation, and listening and speaking skills that you learned in the unit.*

STEP 1: Choose a situation for the role play. Choose from the following ideas:

- filing a police report
- receiving a bill from a department store
- calling a credit card company about a theft
- giving advice to a friend about identity theft
- (your own idea)

Decide on the place, characters, and story. Choose from the following ideas:

Place:

- at a police station
- in a department store
- on the phone
- (your own idea)

Characters (think about age, personality, and feelings about the situation):

- identity theft victim
- police officer
- store employee
- identity thief
- (your own idea)

Story:

- Background: What happened before the role play starts?
- Plot: What happens during the role play?

---

*For Alternative Speaking Topics, see page 49.

STEP 2: Create the role play. Act like your character and speak naturally. Practice the role play several times.

STEP 3: Perform your role play for the class.

Watch the role plays. Which role play did you like best? Discuss with a partner why you liked that role play.

UNIT PROJECT

STEP 1: Find out more about identity theft. Choose one topic from the box or think of your own.

child identity theft	mortgage fraud	skimming
criminal identity theft	phishing	trash theft
data theft	shoulder surfing	

STEP 2: Research the topic on the Internet or in the library, or interview a victim of identity theft. Use the questions to guide your research.

1. What is _____?

2. Is it a common way to commit identity theft?

3. What can people do to protect themselves against _____? Is there any technology that can be used to help people avoid _____?

4. What punishments do criminals receive for _____ _____?

5. What are some other interesting facts about _____?

STEP 3: Share your information with the class.

ALTERNATIVE SPEAKING TOPICS

Discuss one or more of the topics. Use the vocabulary and grammar from the unit.

1. Why would someone want to be an identity thief? What would life as an identity thief be like?

2. Before the Internet was invented, was identity theft possible? How was it different?

3. What new kinds of identity theft might we have to deal with in the future?

GO TO MyEnglishLab TO DISCUSS ONE OF THE ALTERNATIVE TOPICS, WATCH A VIDEO ABOUT IDENTITY THEFT, AND TAKE THE UNIT 2 ACHIEVEMENT TEST.

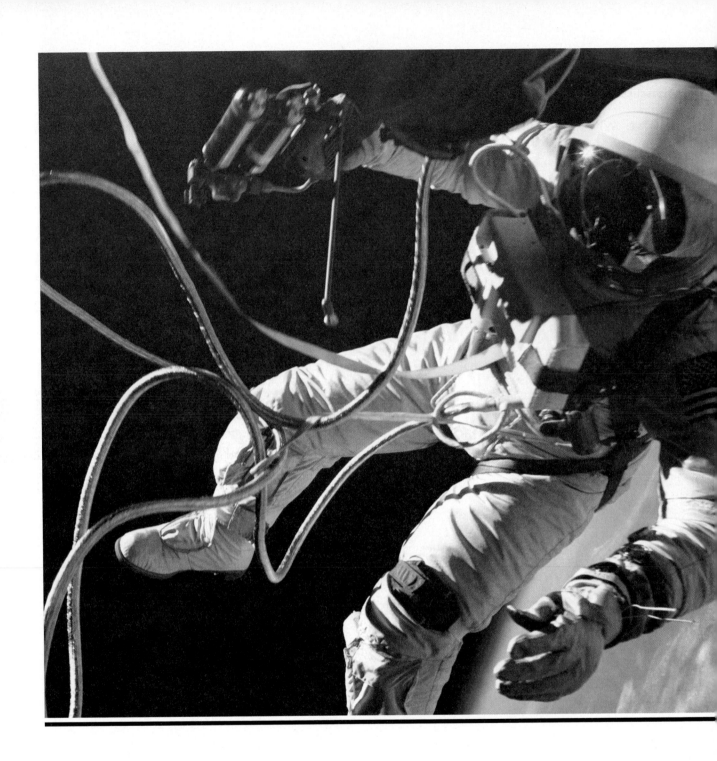

WHY EXPLORE
Space?

1 FOCUS ON THE TOPIC

1. Look at the photo. How do you think it feels to be in space?

2. What kind of space exploration is happening now? What is the purpose of the exploration?

3. What are the benefits of space exploration? What are the risks? Overall, do you think space exploration is a good idea? Why or why not?

GO TO MyEnglishLab *TO CHECK WHAT YOU KNOW.*

LISTENING ONE THE SPACE JUNK PROBLEM

VOCABULARY

1 🎧 Read and listen to an article about a satellite from Ecuador. Notice the boldfaced words.

Ecuador's Satellite Hit by Russian Spacecraft

23 May 2011

An Ecuadorian communication **satellite** was hit by pieces of an old **spacecraft** about 1,500 kilometers (930 miles) above the southeastern coast of Africa. The satellite, called *Pegaso*, was sent into space less than a month ago. It is Ecuador's first satellite to **orbit** Earth.

Scientists knew the satellite would pass near the aging spacecraft, sent up in 1985 by the Soviet Union. The old rocket broke into **fragments** and is now surrounded by a cloud of **debris**. Scientists believe that *Pegaso* **collided** with the debris. The tiny satellite weighed only 1.2 kilograms, so even a small **particle** of debris could have caused **damage**.

Ecuador's space agency EXA said that the satellite continues to orbit but cannot send or receive signals. *Pegaso* was designed to send pictures and video back to Earth. Scientists are **tracking** the satellite to see if it stays on course or stops working completely.

Despite the accident, Ecuador and Russia still plan to **cooperate** on their space programs. Ecuador is planning to send a second satellite into space on a Russian spacecraft in August.

The National Aeronautics and Space Administration (NASA) said that no American satellites are in danger.

Pegaso **Communication Satellite**

2 Match the words with the definitions. Write the words.

damage	fragment	orbit	satellite	track

1. _____: machine that is sent into space and goes around Earth and is used for radio, video, and other electronic communication

2. _____: a piece of something that has broken off something larger

3. _____: physical harm that is done to something

4. _____: to follow the movements of something

5. _____: to travel in a curved path around a much larger object such as the Earth or sun

collide	cooperate	debris	particle	spacecraft

6. _____: a vehicle that is able to travel in space

7. _____: a very small piece of something

8. _____: the pieces of something that are left after it has been destroyed

9. _____: to hit something that is moving in a different direction

10. _____: to work with someone else to do something that you both want

GO TO MyEnglishLab FOR MORE VOCABULARY PRACTICE.

PREVIEW

Trash has been a problem on Earth for many years. Now there is also trash in space. In this radio report, you will learn about space junk.

an orbital debris cloud

damage to the Mir Space Station from space debris

🎧 Listen to an excerpt from the report. Answer the questions from the excerpt.

a. How much space junk[1] is there? _____

b. Is space junk dangerous? _____

---

[1] **junk:** unwanted old objects

MAIN IDEAS

1 🎧 Listen to the whole report. Look again at the questions and your answers from the Preview section. How did they help you understand the report?

2 Complete the statements. Circle the correct answer.

1. Most space debris is created when satellites _____.

   a. stop working

   b. collide or explode

   c. fall back to Earth

2. Debris _____ in a large debris cloud.

   a. orbits Earth

   b. falls to Earth

   c. travels into deep space

3. Falling debris _____.

   a. sometimes causes injury to people on Earth

   b. usually burns up before it reaches the ground

   c. frequently falls into cities and towns

4. Debris fragments in space are dangerous because they _____.

   a. all move in the same direction

   b. orbit close to Earth

   c. travel very fast

5. _____ must cooperate to solve the problem of space debris.

   a. Scientists and researchers

   b. The international community

   c. Governments and businesses

DETAILS

Listen again. Complete each statement. Circle the correct answer.

1. A six-ton piece of space debris the size of a bus fell to Earth in _____.

    a. 2001

    b. 2010

    c. 2011

2. Two events created _____ of the debris in space.

    a. one half (1/2)

    b. one quarter (1/4)

    c. one third (1/3)

3. NASA tracks _____ large debris fragments that orbit Earth.

    a. 2,100

    b. 21,000

    c. 210,000

4. There may be _____ of tiny debris particles.

    a. hundreds

    b. millions

    c. hundreds of millions

5. Each day, an average of _____ of space debris falls to Earth.

    a. one piece

    b. five pieces

    c. ten pieces

6. Space debris travels at _____ kilometers per second.

    a. 8

    b. 8.8

    c. 18

7. There are over _____ working satellites in orbit around Earth.

   a. 1,000

   b. 5,000

   c. 10,000

8. _____ countries formed an organization to solve the problem of space debris.

   a. Two

   b. Twelve

   c. Twenty

⬛⬛⬛⬛⬛⬛⬛⬛⬛⬛⬛⬛⬛⬛⬛⬛⬛⬛⬛⬛⬛⬛⬛⬛⬛⬛⬛⬛⬛⬛⬛⬛⬛⬛⬛⬛ *GO TO* MyEnglishLab *FOR MORE LISTENING PRACTICE.*

MAKE INFERENCES

INFERRING FACTUAL INFORMATION FROM CONTEXT

A speaker may give facts indirectly. The listener can infer the facts based on the context.

🎧 Listen to the excerpt. Notice how Michaela Johnson corrects the reporter. Based on inference, who do you think Michaela Johnson means when she says "we"?

Example

REPORTER:	But this made us wonder: How much space junk is up there? And are we in danger?
MICHAELA JOHNSON:	Well, we call it orbital debris, not space junk.

Michaela Johnson means scientists. She doesn't say directly that scientists use the term "orbital debris." However, you can infer the information from the context because she is a scientist, and she says "we call it . . ."

1 🎧 Listen to the excerpts. What is the inferred meaning of each statement? Complete each statement. Circle the correct answer. Then write the key words from the excerpt that helped you decide.

Excerpt One

NASA can't track most of the debris fragments because they _____.

a. are not important

b. move too fast

c. are too small

Key words: _____

(continued on next page)

People _____ being hit by space debris.

a. should

b. should not worry about

c. should look out for

Key words: _____

_____ are dangerous to spacecraft.

a. Only large fragments

b. Only small fragments

c. Fragments of all sizes

Key words: _____

2 Work with a partner. Talk about the information that helped you find the answers.

EXPRESS OPINIONS

Work in a small group. Discuss the questions.

1. Not all countries send spacecraft and satellites into space, but people around the world benefit from space-based technology such as cell phone service. Therefore, who should pay to clean up space debris? Who should pay if falling space debris injures a person or damages a house?

2. The report described the need for countries to work together to solve the problem of space debris. What can be done about the problem? How can countries cooperate to find a solution?

3. To find a solution to the space debris problem, more people need to be aware of it. Imagine that you are making a television advertisement to educate people about the problem of space debris. What information would you include? What type of images?

▪▪▪▪▪▪▪▪▪▪▪▪▪▪▪▪▪▪▪▪▪▪▪▪▪▪▪▪▪▪▪▪▪▪▪▪ GO TO MyEnglishLab TO GIVE YOUR OPINION ABOUT ANOTHER QUESTION.

VOCABULARY

1 Read the facts about space. Notice the boldfaced words.

Did you know?

1. The first telescope was invented in 1608. Since then, many more **innovations**, from water filters to smoke detectors, have been inspired by space research.

2. Flight **crews** on the International Space Station (ISS) have included people from 15 different countries.

3. In 2002, scientists found signs of ice on Mars. This information has changed our **perspective** on the history of the planet.

4. The United Nations Office of Outer Space Affairs **promotes** the peaceful uses of outer space.

5. Most spacewalks on the International Space Station last between five to seven hours. Time is **precious** during a spacewalk, so the work must be finished quickly.

Telescope

International Space Station

2 Match boldfaced words with the definitions. Write the words.

_____ **a.** groups of people who work together on a boat or aircraft

_____ **b.** new ideas or inventions

_____ **c.** way of thinking about something

_____ **d.** valuable and should not be wasted

_____ **e.** helps something to develop or increase

COMPREHENSION

Listen to an interview with Ray Santos, a scientist who works with the space exploration industry. Label the three main points with the ideas from the box. (There is one extra choice.) Then, under each main point, cross out the supporting detail that is not mentioned.

Curiosity   Innovation   International Cooperation   Scientific Knowledge

1. _Innovation_
   - We have had to solve new problems in space.
   - Space travel has become easier and cheaper.
   - New products have been developed for use on Earth.

2. _____
   - Countries help each other send satellites into space.
   - Countries work together to run the International Space Station.
   - Countries develop positive relationships.

3. _____
   - There is still a lot to find out about space.
   - Space exploration has given us a new perspective.
   - We can look for life on other planets.

GO TO MyEnglishLab FOR MORE VOCABULARY PRACTICE.

LISTENING SKILL

1 🎧 Listen to an excerpt from the interview with Ray Santos. What does the word *it* refer to?

Is **it** worth the price?

PRONOUN REFERENCE

Speakers use pronouns (*it, they, this, that, he, she*) to refer to people, things, and ideas. It is important to understand which people, things, or ideas a speaker is referring to.

A pronoun may refer to something mentioned before or to an idea that is not directly stated.

🎧 Listen to the excerpt. Notice the pronouns in **bold**.

Example

RAY SANTOS:	Space exploration has a lot of benefits. One is innovation. The research for the space program has led to all kinds of innovations.
INTERVIEWER:	Can you tell us about some of **those**?
RAY SANTOS:	Think about **it**: To get into space **we** had to solve all kinds of problems.

- *Those* refers to *innovations*.
- *It* refers to *space exploration*.
- *We* refers to *scientists or people in general*.

2 🎧 Listen to the excerpts. Then write the meaning of the boldfaced words.

Pronoun	Refers to
Excerpt One	
a. *It* has brought together international flight crews	it = _____
b. *This cooperation* promotes positive relationships	this cooperation = cooperation between _____
Excerpt Two	
c. *we*'ve had a great curiosity	we = _____
d. *This curiosity* has led us to explore	this curiosity = curiosity about _____
e. And *it* doesn't just give us answers —*it* gives perspective	it = _____
f. we see how precious *it* is . . .	it = _____

▪▪▪▪▪▪▪▪▪▪▪▪▪▪▪▪▪▪▪▪▪▪▪▪▪▪▪▪▪▪▪▪▪▪▪▪▪▪ *GO TO* MyEnglishLab *FOR MORE SKILL PRACTICE.*

CONNECT THE LISTENINGS

STEP 1: Organize

🎧 Listen to Listenings One and Two again. Then complete the chart with details about the effects of space exploration.

WHAT ARE THE EFFECTS OF SPACE EXPLORATION?		
	LISTENING ONE: **The Space Junk Problem**	**LISTENING TWO:** **The View from Space**
EFFECTS ON INDIVIDUAL PEOPLE	• Space debris falls _____ _____. • Space debris may damage satellites, causing problems with _____ _____.	• It promotes innovation • It gives us _____.
EFFECTS ON COUNTRIES	• Countries must work _____ _____.	• Countries work _____ _____. • The U.S. spends $1.8 billion per year.
EFFECTS IN SPACE	• Space debris damages spacecraft. • Collisions create _____ _____.	

STEP 2: Synthesize

Work in a group of four. Discuss the questions about space exploration. Use the details and examples from Step 1: Organize.

1. What are the positive effects of space exploration?

2. What are the negative effects?

Switch partners and repeat the discussion.

GO TO MyEnglishLab TO CHECK WHAT YOU LEARNED.

VOCABULARY

Read each question and notice the boldfaced word. Then circle the correct answer.

1. What happens when two things **collide**?

    a. They crash.

    b. They go faster.

    c. They turn around.

2. How can countries **cooperate** on the space junk problem?

    a. They can argue about what to do.

    b. They can work together to clean it up.

    c. They can cancel their space programs.

3. A rock hit the space station. What did the **damage** look like?

    a. a small planet

    b. a hole

    c. a piece of metal

4. What should we do with the **debris**?

    a. clean it up

    b. sell it

    c. create more of it

5. Where would you find a flight **crew**?

    a. on a boat

    b. on an airplane

    c. in a nest

(continued on next page)

6. What is a **fragment**?

   a. a piece of a larger object

   b. two pieces of an object joined together

   c. an unbroken object

7. What **innovation** has improved communication?

   a. space

   b. conversation

   c. the Internet

8. What **orbits** the Earth?

   a. the Sun

   b. the moon

   c. planets

9. What does a **particle** look like?

   a. a tiny spot of dirt

   b. a large rock

   c. frozen water

10. What is a person's **perspective**?

    a. how the person sees things

    b. the person's goals

    c. where the person grew up

11. What's an example of something that is **precious**?

    a. a rock from California

    b. a picture of a rock from Mars

    c. a rock from Mars

12. How can you **promote** something?

    a. put it in a safe place

    b. take good care of it

    c. tell people about it

13. Where can you see a **satellite**?

    a. under the ground

    b. in the night sky

    c. at the mall

14. Where might a **spacecraft** go?

    a. to New York

    b. to China

    c. to Mars

15. How do scientists **track** moving objects in the sky?

    a. They discuss them.

    b. They destroy them.

    c. They watch them.

1 Read the article about space tourism. Notice the boldfaced words.

Space Tourism

Have you ever wanted to travel into space? Several companies want to take **commercial** passengers into space—for a price.

There is only one passenger on each flight of the Lynx spacecraft. The passenger sits in front next to the pilot. The spacecraft takes off from the ground like an airplane and then goes almost straight up. After leaving Earth's **atmosphere**, the engines turn off. Outside of Earth's **gravity**, travelers experience weightlessness for about four minutes. They also get an amazing view of Earth. The spacecraft slowly floats back to Earth to land. The cost for the 30-minute flight is $95,000 per person.

Two passengers travel with the pilot in a Soyuz spacecraft for a private **mission** to circle the moon. First, they spend 10 days on the International Space Station before traveling to the moon. Then the spacecraft makes a four-day circle around the moon. It comes within 100 kilometers of the moon's **surface**, giving travelers a view that only a few **astronauts** have seen. Seats on the flight cost $150 million each.

2 Complete the definitions. Write the correct letter.

_____ **1.** A seat on a **commercial** spaceflight is

_____ **2.** Earth's **atmosphere** is

_____ **3.** **Gravity** is

_____ **4.** A **mission** is

_____ **5.** The **surface** is

_____ **6.** An **astronaut** is

a. a person who travels and works in space.

b. a trip by a spacecraft to complete a specific task.

c. sold by a business to make money.

d. the force that causes something to fall to the ground.

e. the mixture of gases that surrounds Earth.

f. the top area of something.

Work in small groups. Make a prediction about the future of space exploration. Agree or disagree with others' predictions. Use at least one of the words from Review and Expand. Use the expressions from the box.

Expressions

In 10 years . . .	there will / won't be _____	announce
In 50 years . . .	the international community will / won't _____	cause
In 100 years . . .	people will / won't _____	create
In the future . . .		send
		solve
		travel

Example

A: In 50 years, people will travel to Mars on commercial missions, as tourists.

B: Maybe, but I don't think there will be enough innovation or money to do that in 50 years.

A: In the future, space flight will become more dangerous. There will be more debris orbiting Earth.

B: Right. That means the debris might collide with the spacecraft.

■■ GO TO MyEnglishLab FOR MORE VOCABULARY PRACTICE.

GRAMMAR

1 What do you know about space? Take the Space Quiz. Check (✓) the statements that are true. Notice the boldfaced verbs.

Space Quiz

☐ **1.** Twelve astronauts **have walked** on the moon.

☐ **2.** Astronomer Carl Sagan's 1980 TV series *Cosmos* **created** popular interest in space.

☐ **3.** NASA **has sent** schoolchildren to the International Space Station.

☐ **4.** In 1970, the *Apollo 13* spacecraft **collided** with a satellite.

☐ **5.** Astronauts **haven't landed** on Venus yet.

Answers: All of the statements are true except #3.

PRESENT PERFECT AND SIMPLE PAST

1. Use the present perfect to talk about things that happened at an indefinite time in the past.	Astronauts **have landed** on the moon. **Have** they **landed** on Mars?
2. Use the present perfect and adverbs like **twice** or **many times** to talk about repeated actions at some time in the past.	The astronaut **has gone** to the International Space Station many times. How many times **has** he **gone** there?
3. Use the present perfect with **not . . . yet** to talk about something that has not happened before now.	Astronauts **haven't traveled** to Mars yet.
4. Use the simple past to talk about things that happened at specific times in the past.	Astronauts first **landed** on the moon in 1969. When **did** they **land** on the moon?

2 Complete the sentences. Write the simple past or the present perfect form of the verbs.

1. More than 55 women astronauts (fly) _____ in space. Most of them (be) _____ born in the United States.

2. (hear) _____ you _____ of Sally Ride? In 1983, she (become) _____ the first American woman to travel in space.

3. Astronaut Sunita Williams (stay) _____ in space for a total of 322 days. She first (go) _____ to the International Space Station in 2007 and stayed for 195 days and then (return) _____ in 2012 and stayed for another 127 days.

4. China (send) _____ female astronauts into space twice: Liu Yang in 2012, and Wang Yaping in 2013. Many space programs (not / send) _____ any female astronauts yet.

5. Last summer our family (visit) _____ the International Women's Air and Space Museum in Ohio. We hope to return next summer, but we (not / decide) _____ yet.

3 Read about the History of the Space Age on the next page. Take turns making statements about the facts, using the simple past and present perfect. Use the verbs from the box.

Example

A: Let's see . . . 60 women **have gone** into space.

B: Right, and the first woman in space **was** Valentina Tereshkova. She **went** into space in 1963.

be	orbit	travel
go	send	walk
land	spend time	

HISTORY OF THE SPACE AGE

The modern Space Age began in 1942 when the first rocket entered outer space. Since then, many new records for space travel have been set.

CATEGORY	TOTAL NUMBER DURING SPACE AGE	FUN FACT
Women in space	More than 55 women	First woman in space: Valentina V. Tereshkova, 1963
Satellites in orbit	thousands of satellites	First satellite to orbit Earth: *Sputnik 1*, 1957
People in space	more than 500 astronauts	First person in space: Yuri Gagarin, 1961
People in space for more than one year	4 people	Longest time in space: Valeri Polyakov, 437 days
People on the moon	12 astronauts	First humans on the moon: crew of the *Apollo 11*, 1969
Spacewalks	More than 130 so far[1]	First spacewalk: 23 minutes, Alexi Leonov, 1965[2] Longest spacewalk: 8 hours 56 minutes, Susan J. Helms and James Voss, 2001
Number of manned spaceflights	About 300 so far	Most spaceflights: 7 trips, Jerry Ross (between 1985–2002) and Franklin Chang-Diaz (between 1986–2002)

GO TO MyEnglishLab *FOR MORE GRAMMAR PRACTICE.*

[1] Spacewalks usually involve two or more people.
[2] Leonov floated in space for about 10 minutes; however, he was outside the spacecraft for at least 20 minutes.

PRONUNCIATION

SIMPLE PAST AND PAST PARTICIPLES: -ED ENDINGS

- The ending -ed is pronounced three ways:
- As /əd/ when the base verb ends in a /t/ or /d/ sound. This adds a syllable.
- As /t/ when the base verb ends in a voiceless sound
- As /d/ when the base verb ends in a vowel or voiced sound

🎧 Listen to the examples and repeat.

Examples

/əd/ : started, decided

/t/ : stopped, worked, passed, watched

/d/ : played, caused, changed, returned, traveled

1 🎧 Listen to the **-ed** sound in the underlined words. Check (✓) the sound you hear.

	/əd/	/t/	/d/
1. The satellite <u>exploded</u>.	☐	☐	☐
2. The debris <u>damaged</u> the spacecraft.	☐	☐	☐
3. Scientists have <u>tracked</u> its orbit for many years.	☐	☐	☐
4. Have they <u>solved</u> the problem yet?	☐	☐	☐
5. Debris <u>surrounded</u> the planet.	☐	☐	☐
6. How many astronauts have <u>walked</u> on the moon?	☐	☐	☐
7. NASA <u>decided</u> to end the program.	☐	☐	☐
8. What <u>caused</u> the damage?	☐	☐	☐
9. They <u>finished</u> the spacewalk in less than an hour.	☐	☐	☐

2 🎧 Listen and repeat the words from Exercise 1.

3 Work with a partner. Take turns asking and answering questions. Use words from the box to complete the conversations. Remember to use *-ed* endings with correct pronunciation.

cause	create	tour	want
collide	injure	visit	work

1. **A:** What happened to the Ecuadoran satellite?

   B: It _____ with an old spacecraft.

2. **A:** Would you like to go into space?

   B: Yes, I've always _____ to be an astronaut. / No, I've never _____ to be an astronaut.

3. **A:** Have you ever _____ the National Air and Space Museum in Washington, D.C.?

   B: Yes, I have. I _____ it in _____ (year). / No, I haven't _____ it.

4. **A:** What was Sally Ride's profession?

   B: She _____ as an astronaut for NASA.

5. **A:** Who _____ the space debris problem?

   B: Every country with a space program has _____ it.

6. **A:** Has space debris ever hurt anyone?

   B: No, it hasn't _____ anyone yet.

SPEAKING SKILL

SUPPORTING YOUR OPINIONS

Read the following blog about space junk. Notice the words and phrases in **bold**.

I think we should stop going into space until we figure out what to do with all the junk we leave up there. **One reason is** that it might come crashing down on us! **For example,** a woman in Texas was hit by a piece of space debris. **She was walking in a park early one morning when a small piece of metal landed on her shoulder.** This is the only time someone has been hit by space junk so far, but it could happen again.

Ways to Support Your Opinions

For a strong opinion, use all three ways to support your idea.

GIVE A REASON	*One reason . . .* *Another reason . . .*	*One reason we should clean up space junk is that it could come crashing down on us.*
	. . . because . . .	*We should clean up space junk because it could come crashing down on us.*
GIVE AN EXAMPLE	*For example . . .* *For instance . . .* *Another example . . .*	*For example, a woman in Texas got hit by a piece of space junk.*
	Let me give an example . . .	*Let me give an example. A woman in Texas got hit by a piece of space junk.*
ELABORATE	(explain in more detail)	*She was walking in a park early one morning when a small piece of metal landed on her shoulder.*

1 Work with a partner. Complete the paragraph with language for supporting an opinion. Underline the sentence that elaborates.

Some people believe that one day humans might be able to live on Mars. One

_____ is that, in important ways, Mars is similar to Earth.

_____, there is water on Mars. Spacecraft on Mars have found ice

on the planet, and scientists believe that there is also a large amount of water underground.

This is an important discovery _____ we have not found water on

any other planet.

2 Work in a small group. Sit in a circle. Read Question A. (1) State your opinion, (2) support your opinion with a reason, and (3) give an example and/or elaborate. Go around the circle so that each student gives an answer. Continue in the same way with the other questions.

Questions

A. Do you agree with the blogger's belief that space junk is a big problem for people on Earth?

B. So far we have only sent robots to Mars, but there are people who want to go. Should we send people even though it could be dangerous?

C. Some companies have started commercial space tourism programs. Do you think this is a good business plan?

D. Should more young people be encouraged to look for careers in space exploration?

GO TO MyEnglishLab FOR MORE SKILL PRACTICE AND TO CHECK WHAT YOU LEARNED.

FINAL SPEAKING TASK

In a small group discussion, people share information and have a conversation about the ideas.

In this activity, you will have two small group discussions about the positive and negative effects of space exploration.

Work in groups. Follow the steps. Try to use the vocabulary, grammar, pronunciation, and listening and speaking skills that you learned in the unit.*

STEP 1: Divide into four groups. Each group will read and discuss the information for *one* of the following topics about the U.S. space program (Student Activities, page 211):

- Finance and Economy
- Environment
- Innovation and Development
- Human Relations

In your group:

1. Read only the information for your topic. (For example, if your topic is "Finance and Economy," read only the information in that section.)

2. Discuss the information and sort it into two categories. Label the information "Positive" or "Negative."

3. Add any other information that you know about your topic, and label it "Positive" or "Negative."

4. Be prepared to explain the information in your own words (without reading) in the next step.

STEP 2: Divide into four new groups. Each group should have an "expert" from one of the four topic areas (one person from Finance and Economy, Environment, Innovation and Development, and Human Relations). Present the information about your topic to the group. After each person presents, discuss the questions.

1. What are the positive effects of the space program?

2. What are the negative effects of the space program?

3. As a group, consider all the information and decide: Is space exploration a good idea? Why or why not?

---

*For Alternative Speaking Topics, see page 77.

STEP 3: One student in each group reports to the class on the group's answer to question 3.

Listening Task

Listen carefully to the information shared by your classmates so that you can express your opinion about the questions.

UNIT PROJECT

There are many exciting projects planned for future space exploration. Some are scientific projects planned by government space agencies, and others are commercial projects planned by private businesses.

STEP 1: Choose a space project to research. You can choose a project from the list below or another similar project.

SUGGESTED TOPICS

NASA Projects

Asteroid[1] Redirect Initiative

Commercial Crew Program

IRIS (Interface Region Imaging Spectograph)

Mars 2020 Mission Plans

LADEE (Lunar Atmosphere Dust Environment Explorer)

International Space Station

Commercial Projects

Asteroid Mining

Space Tourism

Mars One

STEP 2: Research the project. Learn about the project by listening to an online lecture or report, visiting a science museum, visiting an educational website, or doing another type of research. Find out about the goals of the project and the plans for reaching the goals.

STEP 3: Prepare a presentation on the project for your class.

---

[1] **asteroid:** a small rocky object that orbits the sun

ALTERNATIVE SPEAKING TOPICS

Discuss one of the topics. Use the vocabulary and grammar from the unit.

1. Some people are interested in business opportunities in space. One idea is to start a space tourism business and charge money to take people into space. Another idea is to get minerals and metals from asteroids and sell them on Earth.

   a. Do you think it is a good idea to allow companies to use space for commercial purposes? Why or why not?

2. People have wondered if there is other intelligent life in the universe. Although we have not found any extraterrestrials[1] yet, scientists have found other planets that could support life. We have tried to send messages into space and listened to signals from other planets, but so far there has been no communication.

   a. Do you think it is a good idea to look for extraterrestrials? Should we try to communicate with them? Why or why not?

   b. There are many images of extraterrestrials in movies, TV shows, and books. If we found real extraterrestrials, do you think they would be similar to those fictional beings?

GO TO MyEnglishLab TO DISCUSS ONE OF THE ALTERNATIVE TOPICS, WATCH A VIDEO ABOUT SPACE, AND TAKE THE UNIT 3 ACHIEVEMENT TEST.

---

[1] **extraterrestrial:** living being from another planet

WORDS THAT
Persuade

1 FOCUS ON THE TOPIC

1. Look at the photo. What do you think the salesman will say to persuade a customer to buy a car?

2. There is a saying that "A good salesperson can sell you what you need. A great salesperson can sell you what you don't want and can't afford." Think of a time when a salesperson persuaded you (or someone you know) to buy something. What did the salesperson say? Why was it persuasive?

3. Advertising uses language to persuade us to buy a product. For example, many ads say that a product is "new" or "improved." With the class, brainstorm a list of words or phrases that you commonly see or hear in advertisements. Why are they persuasive?

GO TO MyEnglishLab TO CHECK WHAT YOU KNOW.

VOCABULARY

1 🎧 Read and listen to the article about how we use language. Notice the boldfaced words.

○ ○ ○

Watch Your Language: For people who love languages
Fool[1] Me Once

Most people like to think that they are truthful, but studies show that, in reality, adults often tell "little white lies"—small, harmless lies—in social situations. For example, if a friend cooks dinner and asks, "How do you like it?," most people will say, "It's delicious," even if they think it tastes terrible. In this **context**, a lie is acceptable because it is used to avoid hurting someone's feelings.

People also use **euphemisms** to avoid hurting people's feelings. Euphemisms are polite words or expressions that people use to talk about—and around—upsetting or embarrassing topics. For example, many people feel uncomfortable talking **directly** about death, so they use euphemisms. They might say "pass away" instead of "die." "Pass away" is less upsetting because it suggests that death is only a **transition** to another place.

In the business world, advertisers use euphemisms to sell products that solve embarrassing problems. For example, one company advertises mouthwash for "morning breath," which has a much better **connotation** than the more common term "bad breath." By using the positive image of a new morning instead of the negative word "bad," the euphemism promotes a more positive feeling about the product.

While most white lies and euphemisms have no real victims, some language can be used to hide the truth and can be quite **deceptive**.

Take the advertising expression "new and improved." We see this everywhere. It makes us think that we are paying for a better product, but the only difference is a change in the packaging.

Deceptive language is also found in the **corporate** world. A recent news report quoted the head of a large business as saying, "The company experienced a significant **reduction** last year." What he really meant was, "We lost money and **fired** a lot of people." The statement influences our opinion of the company by hiding the true financial situation.

There is an **excessive** amount of deceptive language in the world today. Why? Because it works! But, as the expression goes, Fool me once, shame on you. Fool me twice, shame on me. As language lovers, we can be smarter by learning to listen closely to the words we hear.

---

[1] **fool:** to trick someone into believing something that is not true

2 Circle the best definition for each word.

1. context

    a. the situation or information that helps you to understand something

    b. the situation or information that makes you confused about something

2. euphemism

    a. a lie used to hurt someone

    b. a polite word or expression used to make something less unattractive

3. directly

    a. say something without being clear

    b. say exactly what you mean

4. transition

    a. when a person stays in the same situation

    b. when a person changes from one situation to another

5. connotation

    a. a positive or negative feeling suggested by a word

    b. the basic meaning of a word

6. deceptive

    a. intended to make someone believe something that is not true

    b. intended to tell the truth about something

7. excessive

    a. much more than necessary

    b. not enough

8. corporate

    a. relating to a big company or a group of companies

    b. relating to individual people

(continued on next page)

9. reduction

    a. a decrease in size or amount

    b. an increase in size or amount

10. fire

    a. to force someone to leave a job

    b. to give someone a new job

■■■ GO TO MyEnglishLab FOR MORE VOCABULARY PRACTICE.

PREVIEW

A businessman gives an online lecture about euphemisms used in the corporate world.

🎧 Listen to an excerpt from the lecture. What do you think is the purpose of this lecture? Circle your prediction.

a. To argue in favor of using corporate euphemisms

b. To compare corporate and non-corporate euphemisms

c. To explain why people use corporate euphemisms

MAIN IDEAS

1 🎧 Listen to the whole lecture. Look again at your prediction from the Preview section. How did your prediction help you understand the lecture?

2 Complete each statement. Circle the correct answer.

1. Euphemisms are _____ used in the corporate world.

    a. often

    b. seldom

    c. never

2. Businesses try to _____ words with negative connotations.

    a. create

    b. avoid

    c. use

3. The same euphemisms are often used _____.

    a. at work and with friends

    b. in different contexts

    c. in more than one conversation

4. Over time, euphemisms can become more _____.

    a. meaningful

    b. useful

    c. negative

5. Doublespeak is language that _____.

    a. hides the truth

    b. is honest and clear

    c. confuses the speaker

DETAILS

Listen again. Fill in the missing information.

1. *Workforce reduction* is a corporate euphemism for _____.

2. *Sanitation worker* is a euphemism for _____.

3. _____ means the removal of dirt to protect public health.

4. *Between jobs* and *going through a career transition* are euphemisms for _____.

5. *Funemployed* is an example of a euphemism you use with _____, not employers.

(continued on next page)

Words That Persuade   83

6. *Downsizing* is a corporate euphemism for _____.

7. _____ is an example of a euphemism that got a negative connotation over time.

8. Using 29 different euphemisms to mean "fire people" is an example of _____.

GO TO MyEnglishLab FOR MORE LISTENING PRACTICE.

MAKE INFERENCES

INFERRING SPEAKER PURPOSE

A speaker may have a specific purpose for making a statement. For example, the speaker may want to define a new term, contrast two ideas, or persuade the listener to agree with an idea. The listener can infer the speaker's purpose by paying attention to the context.

It is important to be able to identify the purpose of each statement so that you can understand the speaker's overall intended meaning.

🎧 Listen to an excerpt from the lecture. What is the speaker's purpose when he makes the statement in **bold**?

Example

> A friend of mine got a letter from his employer that said the company was having a "workforce reduction" because of "changes in the market environment." What they really mean is that **a bunch of people are going to be fired because the company is in financial trouble**.

The purpose of the statement is to define the terms *workforce reduction* and *changes in the market environment*. The speaker says the new terms slowly and carefully, and then he explains what they mean.

1 🎧 Listen to the excerpts. What is the speaker's purpose? Read each statement. Circle the correct answer.

Excerpt One

What is the speaker's purpose when he says ". . . he's out of a job but now has the time to do fun things during the work week"?

a. to define the term *funemployed*

b. to contrast *funemployed* and *unemployed*

c. to persuade the listener that *funemployed* is a useful euphemism

What is the speaker's purpose when he says "However, over the years, it's become just as bad—just like saying 'we're firing people.' The connotation is the same now!"

a. to define the term *downsizing*

b. to contrast *downsizing* and *firing people*

c. to persuade the listener that *downsizing* has a negative connotation

What is the speaker's purpose when he says, "Twenty-nine—in one page! That's too much—people get angry at this kind of doublespeak. They want to be told the truth, not hear euphemisms that hide the truth"?

a. to define the term *doublespeak*

b. to contrast *doublespeak* and *euphemism*

c. to persuade the listener that using doublespeak is a bad idea

2 Work with a partner. Talk about the information that helped you find the answers.

EXPRESS OPINIONS

Work in small groups. Choose a set of questions to discuss.

1. When is it OK to use euphemisms or deceptive language in a corporate context? When is it not OK? What about euphemisms or deceptive language in personal relationships?

2. Are corporate euphemisms used in your native language? How are the expressions similar to or different from the euphemisms mentioned in the lecture?

3. When do you use euphemisms? What are some examples? Why do you use them?

■■■■■■■■■■■■■■■■■■■■■■■■■■■■■ GO TO MyEnglishLab *TO GIVE YOUR OPINION ABOUT ANOTHER QUESTION.*

VOCABULARY

1 Complete the Internet survey. Notice the boldfaced words.

○ ○ ○

What's your style?
Before you start looking for a new home, take this quiz!

1. I like rooms that have . . .
- ○ high ceilings and a lot of space
- ○ a **cozy**, warm feeling

2. I prefer furniture that has . . .
- ○ a **vintage** look from the 60s or 70s
- ○ a modern, up-to-date style

3. I like colors that are . . .
- ○ **vibrant** and bright
- ○ soft and pale

4. I'm looking for a house that . . .
- ○ needs some repairs and updates
- ○ doesn't need any **maintenance**

5. In the kitchen, I want . . .
- ○ a **compact** refrigerator that doesn't take up too much room
- ○ a large refrigerator that holds a lot of food

2 Match the boldfaced words with the definitions. Write the words.

_____ **a.** designed to be small and not waste space

_____ **b.** full of activity or energy in a way that is exciting and attractive

_____ **c.** old, but high quality

_____ **d.** the repairs that are necessary to keep something in good condition

_____ **e.** small and comfortable

COMPREHENSION

Listen to an episode from the TV series "Home Sweet Home." In this scene, a real estate agent gives a client a tour of a house. Fill in the missing information.

The euphemism . . .	**What the client thinks . . .**
1. The living room is cozy.	The living room is _____.
2. The neighborhood is vibrant.	The neighborhood is _____.
3. The kitchen is compact and well organized.	The kitchen is _____.
4. The cabinets have a vintage look.	The cabinets are _____.
5. The backyard is low maintenance.	The backyard has no _____.
6. The apartment is "not going to work for me."	"I _____ the apartment."

GO TO MyEnglishLab FOR MORE VOCABULARY PRACTICE.

LISTENING SKILL

1 🎧 Listen to an excerpt from "Home Sweet Home." Is the real estate agent making strong positive statements, or is she making polite negative comments? What word emphasizes her point?

LISTENING FOR SPEAKER EMPHASIS

Intensifiers are adverbs used to emphasize another word. Speakers use intensifiers to make a point sound stronger. They can also use intensifiers to make a point less strong. This makes a negative idea sound more polite.

🎧 Read and listen to the examples:

Example

REAL ESTATE AGENT: Well, it's a compact kitchen. It's **very** well organized.

CLIENT: Those cabinets are **sort of** old-fashioned.

2 🎧 Listen to the excerpts. Complete the statement with the intensifier you hear. Does the intensifier make the statement sound stronger or more polite? Circle the correct answer.

Excerpt One

It has some _____ great features.

The intensifier makes the statement   **a.** stronger   **b.** more polite

Excerpt Two

It seems _____ small.

The intensifier makes the statement   **a.** stronger   **b.** more polite

Excerpt Three

I'd _____ put the sofa over here along this wall . . .

The intensifier makes the statement   **a.** stronger   **b.** more polite

Excerpt Four

But it's _____ small, too.

The intensifier makes the statement   **a.** stronger   **b.** more polite

GO TO MyEnglishLab FOR MORE SKILL PRACTICE.

STEP 1: Organize

Listen to Listenings One and Two again. Then complete the chart with details about euphemisms.

	LISTENING ONE: Corporate Euphemisms	LISTENING TWO: House Hunting
EUPHEMISMS ARE USED BY:	_____ people looking for a job	_____
EUPHEMISMS USED TO MAKE SOMETHING SOUND BETTER:	fire people = _____ = _____*downsize*_____ garbage collector = _____ unemployed = _____ = _____ = _____	small = _____ = _____ busy / noisy = _____ old-fashioned = _____ no grass = _____ I don't like it = _*it's not going to work for*_ _*me. . . .*_

STEP 2: Synthesize

Work in groups of four. Each person in the group speaks from a different point of view: a corporate leader, an employee, a real estate agent, a home buyer. Take turns completing each statement and giving an example from Step 1: Organize.

Statements

a. I think that euphemisms (hurt people / make people feel better). For example, . . .

b. I think that euphemisms (are necessary / are used too much) in business. For example, . . .

c. I think that euphemisms (are deceptive / make negative ideas sound more positive). For example, . . .

GO TO MyEnglishLab TO CHECK WHAT YOU LEARNED.

VOCABULARY

REVIEW

Cross out the meaning that doesn't match the boldfaced word. Consult a dictionary if necessary.

1. The TV commercial shows the new Micro, which is a **compact** car that easily fits into a tight parking space.

   a. small and well organized

   b. ~~fast~~

2. The word *spam* has a negative **connotation**, while *advertisement* is more neutral.

   a. dictionary definition of a word

   b. feeling about a word

3. The billboard reads "Don't!" above a burning cigarette. The cigarette provides the **context** for understanding the message.

   a. the situation or information that helps you understand

   b. a book that explains a situation or information

4. The **corporate** world relies on advertising to sell products.

   a. business

   b. entertainment

5. The ad describes the apartment as "**cozy**," which means his large piano won't fit.

   a. small and comfortable

   b. sunny and cheerful

6. The salesman was being **deceptive** when he said the car is in "excellent condition."

   a. truthful

   b. dishonest

7. The commercial doesn't **directly** say what Milagrow is for, but the images show men with no hair.

   a. in a clear way

   b. secretively

8. Advertisements use **euphemisms** to sell things that are embarrassing to talk about.

   a. polite words

   b. pictures

9. There's an **excessive** number of pop-up ads on that website. It's annoying.

   a. not enough

   b. much more than necessary

10. When Kate's boss said he was "letting her go," she didn't understand that she was being **fired**.

    a. given a better job

    b. forced to leave a job

11. **Low-maintenance** clients are the best—they don't complain or need a lot of attention.

    a. requiring a lot of help

    b. needing little to stay satisfied

12. Because of budget **reductions**, the company had to close several offices.

    a. decreases

    b. increases

13. Advertisers quickly made the **transition** from TV, newspapers, and magazines to the Internet.

    a. a change from one situation to another

    b. a payment for services

(continued on next page)

14. The real estate agent said the orange walls in the kitchen were "**vibrant**," but Sara and Max thought the color was horrible.

    a. soft, relaxing, cool

    b. bright, lively, happy

15. Be careful when shopping for "**vintage**" furniture—sometimes the furniture is new and just made to look old.

    a. made of wood and inexpensive

    b. made a long time ago and high quality

EXPAND

1 Read the advertisements.

HOT DEALS!	Everything MUST go!	Smart buy!
Fantastic bargain!	Time is running out!	Buy now and save!

2 Write the words in the box from the advertisements in the correct categories.

Buy quickly: _____

Low price: _____

Both: _____

3 Do you think these expressions are an example of manipulative language or are they truthful statements? Discuss your answers with the class.

CREATE

1 Work with a partner. Choose a context from the bulleted list. Create a short conversation using the words or phrases from the lists. Each word is a different number of points. Try to get as many points as you can.

Contexts

- An employer talking to an employee about changes at the company.

- Two corporate executives discussing how to tell their employees about a workforce reduction.

- A real estate agent trying to sell a house to a client.

- A salesperson trying to sell something to a customer.

- Your idea . . .

1 point	2 points	3 points
compact	buy now and save	context
corporate	everything must go	euphemism
deceptive	fantastic bargain	low maintenance
directly	hot deal	positive / negative connotation
excessive	smart buy	transition
vintage	time is running out	workforce reduction

Example

STUDENT A: This chair is a <u>fantastic bargain</u>! [2 points]

STUDENT B: It would go nicely with my <u>vintage</u> couch. [1 point]

STUDENT A: The sale ends today, so <u>time is running out</u>! [2 points]

2 Perform your conversation for the class. The class tries to guess the context and identify the three words or phrases you used.

GRAMMAR

1 Look at the picture and answer the questions. Notice the boldfaced **superlative adjectives**.

WINTER'S CHILL	7:00	10:00
SUMMER FUN	6:45	8:15
SPRING SONG	7:30	9:00

ADULTS $10   SENIORS $8   CHILDREN $6

1. Which person has the **the longest wait** in line?

   a. the woman at the ticket window

   b. the man in the green hat

   c. the woman with the purse

2. Which ticket is **the most expensive**?

   a. adults

   b. seniors

   c. children

3. Which movie has **the latest** show time?

   a. *Winter's Chill*

   b. *Summer Fun*

   c. *Spring Song*

SUPERLATIVE ADJECTIVES

1. Use superlative adjectives to compare one person, place, or thing with two or more people, places, or things.	*We have* **the lowest** *prices on golf clubs in the area.* *This is* **the best** *printer on the market today!*
Use the superlative to describe something that is more than other things.	cheap—**the cheapest** furniture easy—**the easiest** solution
Use the superlative to describe something that is much less than other things.	expensive—**the least expensive** car amazing—**the most amazing** resort
There are some irregular superlatives.	a **good** deal—**the best** deal a **bad** location—**the worst** location
2. Superlatives are often followed by phrases with **in** or **of**.	*Martinelli's has* **the cheapest** *deals* <u>*in town*</u>. *Our watches are* **the best quality** <u>*of any watches on the market*</u>.

2 Complete the sentences. Write superlatives using the boldfaced adjectives. Some of the sentences may have more than one answer. Then work with a partner and compare answers.

1. This tablet computer is **large**. It is _____ tablet in the store.

2. Dave is a very **knowledgeable** salesperson. Of everyone who works here, he is the

   _____.

3. People don't like corporate doublespeak because it is **manipulative**. In fact, it is often

   _____ type of corporate communication.

4. My new shoes are **stylish** but not expensive. In fact, they are

   _____ of all the shoes I own.

5. All the rooms are painted with **vibrant** colors, but the yellow living room is

   _____.

6. I've seen a few **good** movies lately, but _____ movie was
   Winter's Chill.

(continued on next page)

7. I want an apartment that is not **noisy**, and I think this is _____ apartment I've visited.

8. All restaurants in Westport serve **delicious** food, but I think the food at Marigold is

_____.

3 With your partner, take turns talking about the features you like most and least in each living room. Use superlative adjectives. Use words from the list or think of your own.

Example

STUDENT A: I like Room 2 because it's **the biggest** room. But Room 1 is **the coziest**.

Room 1

Room 2

Room 3

Talk about the . . .	Use the adjectives . . .
decorations	attractive
furniture	colorful
pillows	comfortable
room	cozy
sofa and chairs	good
view	interesting
walls	large
	modern
	vibrant

GO TO MyEnglishLab FOR MORE GRAMMAR PRACTICE.

PRONUNCIATION

HIGHLIGHTING

In radio, TV, and Internet ads, actors emphasize, or *highlight*, certain words to get the listener to focus on important information. The same pattern also occurs in everyday communication. When we speak, we stress key words to make our meaning clear.

To highlight, or emphasize, a word:

- Say the word with a higher pitch (tone).
- Say the word louder.
- Make the word longer.

🎧 Listen to an excerpt from Listening Two. Notice how the boldfaced words sound.

Example

This is the living room. It has some really **great** features. Look at the **nice** wood floors and the **big** windows.

1 Read the transcript from an infomercial for Mistyland, a vacation resort. Circle the words that you think will be highlighted.

WIFE: I just love Mistyland. Our condo is so cozy and clean.

HUSBAND: And low maintenance. There's nothing to do!

WIFE: In fact, the only thing you can do at Mistyland is relax.

HUSBAND: And it has the most amazing golf course! I've never seen such vibrant green grass.

WIFE: Or such beautiful blue skies. This place is absolutely dreamy!

HUSBAND: Come to Mistyland—for your dream vacation.

2 🎧 Listen to the infomercial and check your answers. Compare your answers with a partner's.

3 Work with a partner. Role-play the infomercial. Highlight the words you circled.

SPEAKING SKILL

USING EMOTIONAL APPEALS

Advertisers use *emotional appeals* to persuade people to buy a product. An emotional appeal can be positive, emphasizing positive emotions like happiness or love. It can also be negative, emphasizing negative emotions like fear or embarrassment.

Look at the ad. Underline the words that persuade people to buy the product.

Example

There are several ways to make a product description more persuasive:

Use expressive adjectives	
Example: fantastic, incredible, amazing, awesome, beautiful, outstanding, unbelievable, terrible, disgusting, smelly, dirty, smooth, vibrant, vintage, compact	Lux Face Cream makes skin look incredible and protects your face from the damaging sun.
Use superlatives (see Grammar p. 95)	
Example: smallest, cheapest, fastest, easiest, longest, strongest, most impressive, most reliable, most affordable, most effective, best, worst	Lux Face Cream makes skin look incredible. It is the most effective way to protect your face from the damaging sun.
Add intensifiers (see Listening Skill p. 88)	
Example: very, really, truly, extremely, awfully, definitely, more	Lux Face Cream makes skin look truly incredible. It is the most effective way to protect your face from the damaging sun.

1 Work in groups of four. Make the sentences more persuasive. Student A reads sentence 1 from the list. Student B adds an adjective. Student C adds a superlative. Student D adds an intensifier. Take turns being Student A, Student B, Student C, and Student D.

Example

STUDENT A: This car is good for city driving. (sentence)

STUDENT B: This **powerful** car is good for city driving. (expressive adjective)

STUDENT C: This powerful car is **the most economical** for city driving. (superlative)

STUDENT D: This powerful car is **really** the most economical for city driving. (intensifier)

Sentences

1. This restaurant has food.

2. We have clothes and cheap prices.

3. Come to the sale at the toy shop in town.

4. This travel business arranges vacations for tourists.

5. The fish is fresh and affordable.

2 Work in pairs. Look at the pictures of the products. Create a short advertisement for each product with an expressive adjective, a superlative, and an intensifier. Use a dictionary to help you find new vocabulary. Then share your most persuasive description with the class.

A

Test drive <u>the **incredible** X-14. It's the **most reliable sporty**</u> car on the road.

B

She . . .

(continued on next page)

C

Nobody likes . . .

D

Try . . .

E

Your baby . . .

F

These shoes . . .

GO TO MyEnglishLab FOR MORE SKILL PRACTICE AND TO CHECK WHAT YOU LEARNED.

FINAL SPEAKING TASK

Advertisements are created to persuade people to buy a product by using euphemisms and emotional appeals.

In this activity, you will create and perform a TV, radio, or Internet ad that uses persuasive language, including euphemisms and emotional appeals.

Work in a group. Follow the steps. Try to use the vocabulary, grammar, pronunciation, and listening and speaking skills that you learned in the unit.*

STEP 1: Plan the ad

- Choose a product from the list below or think of your own.

Products that solve an embarrassing problem	Products with a problem
wrinkle cream	used car
acne cream	compact car
diet pills	used cell phone
hair growth medicine	a very expensive product
hair dye	
mouthwash	
deodorant	
dandruff shampoo	

- Decide on a situation for the ad (for example, two people talking in a grocery store).

STEP 2: Write a script and practice the ad

- Write the script together. Use euphemisms and emotional appeals to sell the product.
- Keep the ad short (about 60 seconds).
- Make sure each group member has a speaking part and a copy of the script.
- Practice the script. Be dramatic (show the emotion) and use props (real objects) if you can.

STEP 3: Present the ad to the class. Give a brief introduction about the product. Then perform the ad. As you perform, use highlighting to emphasize key words.

---

*For Alternative Speaking Topics, see page 103.

As you listen to the presentations, take notes on the questions.

1. What product is this ad selling?

2. What persuasive language does this ad use?

As a class, vote to choose the most persuasive ad.

UNIT PROJECT

To be a smart consumer, it is important to be able to analyze and understand how advertising affects us. In this project, you will analyze advertisements to understand the persuasive techniques used to sell products.

There are many persuasive advertising techniques:

- **Euphemism:** Advertisements use positive and negative language to appeal to emotions and persuade people to buy a product.
- **Hype:** The advertisement uses exciting language (adjectives, comparatives, intensifiers) to persuade people to buy.
- **Association:** The advertisement links the product with something that people like, such as a soda commercial that shows a happy family drinking the soda or a car advertisement that shows the car driving along a beautiful road.
- **Testimonial:** People describe how the product helped them. Testimonials can come from everyday customers, celebrities, or experts like doctors.
- **Repetition:** An advertisement is repeated over and over, which makes us remember the product.
- **Humor:** Funny advertisements catch our attention, and the humor makes us feel good.

STEP 1: Find two advertisements for the same type of product, but from two different companies. For example, find advertisements for a car from Honda and Ford. The ads can be in a magazine, on television or radio, or on the Internet.

STEP 2: Analyze the advertisements.

- What is the product?
- Who is the target audience of the ad (men, women, children, older adults, etc.)?
- Write down the words and dialog (written and spoken) that are used in the ad. How is language used to persuade?
- What persuasive techniques are used in the ads?

STEP 3: Work in a small group. Take turns presenting your analysis of the ads. If possible, show the ads to the group. After everyone has shared their analysis, discuss the questions:

- What persuasive techniques are used to sell the different products sold? Do any products use the same techniques?

- Why do you think the company chose the techniques to sell their products and not other techniques? Could other techniques also be effective?

- Do you think any of the ads are deceptive? Why or why not?

ALTERNATIVE SPEAKING TOPICS

In addition to euphemism and doublespeak, here are more types of language used in certain contexts:

jargon: words and expressions used in a particular profession or by a particular group of people, which are difficult for other people to understand

In police jargon, a police car is called a *unit*, and an ambulance is called a *bus*.

slang: very informal language that is used by a particular group, such as young people or criminals

When a teenager says "I'm going to score some kicks," he means "I'm going to get some shoes."

exaggeration: a statement that makes something seem bigger or better than it really is

She said there were "a million" people waiting in line for tickets, but we only had to wait a few minutes to get to the ticket window.

buzzword: a word or phrase from one special area of knowledge that people suddenly think is very important

Multimedia has been a buzzword in the computer industry for years.

Discuss the questions as a class.

1. What is the purpose of each of these different types of language? In what contexts are they used? Can you think of some more examples?

2. Does your native language include any of these types of language? If so, which ones?

3. In your native language, are there any other special ways of speaking that are not listed above? What are they? In what context are they used?

GO TO MyEnglishLab *TO DISCUSS ONE OF THE ALTERNATIVE TOPICS, WATCH A VIDEO ABOUT GENDER AND COMMUNICATION, AND TAKE THE UNIT 4 ACHIEVEMENT TEST.*

FOLLOW YOUR Passion

1 FOCUS ON THE TOPIC

1. A *passion* is an activity that you love to do. Look at the photo. What is this man's passion?

2. More and more people are "following their passions" when they choose careers. What are the advantages of choosing a career that you love? What could be some disadvantages?

3. In order to follow your passion, you first need to know what your passion is. What can you do to "find your passion"?

GO TO MyEnglishLab TO CHECK WHAT YOU KNOW.

VOCABULARY

1 🎧 Read and listen to some myths and facts about college and careers. Notice the boldfaced words and the footnote.

College and Career Myths[1] and Facts

MYTH #1: I want to change my **major** from math to biology, but I think it's too late.

FACT: Don't worry. About 70 percent of college students change their major. If your major isn't right for you, it's fine to **enroll** in another department next year.

MYTH #2: I should only take classes that prepare me for my future career.

FACT: Not true! Employers often look for people with a range of experiences. Don't get **tunnel vision**. Take a class outside of your major. Who knows, you might find a new talent!

MYTH #3: Choosing a major in college means deciding my career for the rest of my life.

FACT: Not so! Many college graduates get jobs that are not directly related to their major, and most will have one or more career **shifts** during their working lives.

MYTH #4: If I don't like college, I can **drop out**, start my own business, and become a billionaire.

FACT: This worked for Facebook founder Mark Zuckerberg, but most American billionaires are college graduates. So if you want to be a billionaire, the best **strategy** is to graduate from college first.

MYTH #5: I shouldn't tell my professor that I'm having trouble in class.

FACT: Actually, most instructors want to be **supportive** of students who are having difficulties in class. Make an appointment with your instructor and ask for help.

MYTH #6: College is much harder than high school.

FACT: Not necessarily. College is "different," but not always "harder." College students have more freedom, so time **management** is important. Plan your time to make sure you get your work done.

For parents . . .
MYTH #7: My child isn't getting good grades. If I offer him money or some other **bribe**, that might encourage him to work harder.

FACT: Bad idea! Giving rewards is not the best way to encourage good grades. Talk to your child about the problem, but a student is **ultimately** responsible for his or her own success.

---
[1]**myth:** an idea that is not true

2 Match the words with the definitions. Write the correct letter.

_____ 1. major

_____ 2. enroll

_____ 3. tunnel vision

_____ 4. shift

_____ 5. drop out

_____ 6. strategy

_____ 7. supportive

_____ 8. management

_____ 9. bribe

_____ 10. ultimately

a. to offer a person something special in order to make the person do something

b. the main subject that a student studies at college or university

c. the act of controlling and organizing someone's work or time

d. to officially join a school, university, or course

e. to change

f. a planned series of actions for achieving something

g. giving help or encouragement

h. thinking about one part of a plan or problem instead of considering all the parts

i. finally, after everything else has been done or considered

j. to leave school before you finish a course

■■ GO TO MyEnglishLab FOR MORE VOCABULARY PRACTICE.

PREVIEW

In these interviews, two professionals talk about the role their parents played in each one's choice of career.

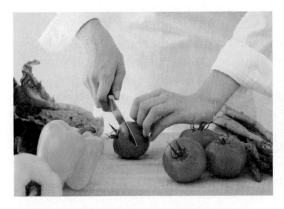 

Julie Hession is a cookbook author and founder of a company that makes breakfast cereal. She has developed her career by blogging about food, participating in cooking contests, and starting food companies.

Simon Sinek is an author and public speaker who teaches leaders and organizations how to inspire[1] people. He is the author of *Start with Why: How Great Leaders Inspire Everyone to Take Action.*

🎧 Listen to excerpts from the interviews. Make predictions.

1. Do you think Julie's father was supportive of her career change? Why or why not?

   _____

2. Do you think Simon's parents were supportive of his career change? Why or why not?

   _____

MAIN IDEAS

1 🎧 Listen to all of both interviews. Look again at your predictions from the Preview section. How did your predictions help you understand the interviews?

2 Circle the correct name to complete each statement.

1. **Julie / Simon** studied hotel and restaurant management.

2. **Julie / Simon** went to law school.

3. **Julie / Simon** was unhappy in her / his first job.

---

[1] **inspire:** to encourage someone to do or produce something good

4. **Julie's / Simon's** father advised changing jobs.

5. **Julie's / Simon's** parents advised finishing school.

6. **Julie / Simon** followed her / his parents' advice.

DETAILS

🎧 Listen again. Read the statements. Write **T** (true) or **F** (false).

_____ 1. In college, Julie learned about a lot of different careers.

_____ 2. Julie's first job was at a hotel in a city where she didn't know anyone.

_____ 3. Julie felt that she had to follow the career she prepared for in college.

_____ 4. Julie's father wanted her to find a career that made more money.

_____ 5. Simon wanted to be a lawyer.

_____ 6. Simon's parents tried a lot of strategies to make him stay in school.

_____ 7. Simon's father encouraged him to change his major.

_____ 8. Simon's parents were ultimately supportive of his decision to quit law school.

GO TO MyEnglishLab FOR MORE LISTENING PRACTICE.

MAKE INFERENCES

INFERRING MEANING FROM CONTEXT

A speaker may express an idea indirectly. The listener can infer the meaning based on the context.

🎧 Listen to the example. What does Julie mean when she says, "I know that's a huge phrase right now . . . but I heard that from my dad a long time ago."?

Example

JULIE: My dad is the first person that ever told me to "follow your passion" and, you know, make money off of it. And I've always, I know that's a huge phrase right now, you hear that all the time, but I heard that from my dad a long time ago.

Here Julie is saying that her dad believed in "following your passion" before the idea became popular. Julie is saying that her father is wise and that she respects his advice.

---

1 🎧 Listen to the excerpts. Read each question. Then complete the statement. Circle the correct answer.

Excerpt One

What does Julie mean when she says, "This is going to be my life."?

I _____ change my career.

    a. can't

    b. don't want to

    c. plan to

Excerpt Two

What does Julie mean when she says, ". . . that was . . . such an *ah-ha* moment for me."?

That was the moment that I _____.

    a. realized something important

    b. felt so sad about my life

    c. was angry with my father

What does Simon mean when he says "And I never fought so much with my parents than during this time."?

During this time, I fought with my parents _____ in the past.

    a. less than

    b. more than

    c. the same amount as

What does Simon mean when he says, ". . . and he says to me, 'So?'"

My dad asked me, _____

    a. "How can I change your mind?"

    b. "What are you going to do?"

    c. "When are you coming home?"

2 Work with a partner. Talk about the information that helped you find the answers.

EXPRESS OPINIONS

Discuss the questions with the class.

    1. Do you think that Julie's and Simon's parents gave good advice? Why or why not?

    2. Do you think Julie and Simon each made the right decision? Why or why not?

GO TO MyEnglishLab TO GIVE YOUR OPINION ABOUT ANOTHER QUESTION.

VOCABULARY

1 Read the summary about a speech you will hear. Notice the boldfaced words.

What is your "passion"? Do you play sports in your spare time? Do you **volunteer** to help people at a school or organization? Do you love to play music?

Some people **take a chance** and follow their passion into a new career. In his talk, Jeremy Benzen describes how he went through a **process** of evaluating his work **environment**, finding his passion, and **figuring out** a new direction in life.

2 Match the words with the definitions. Write the correct letter. Then circle the correct word or phrase to complete the definition.

_e_   **1.** environment

a. to do something **for money / without expecting money**

____   **2.** volunteer

b. **a series of actions / one action** done to get a result

____   **3.** process

c. to do something **risky / safe**

____   **4.** take a chance

d. to **think about / ask for help with** a problem until you find a solution

____   **5.** figure out

e. the (situations) / decisions that affect the way we live and work

COMPREHENSION

1 🎧 Listen to a speech by Jeremy Benzen as he gives advice about how to find your passion in life. Then answer the questions.

Check (✓) the three strategies that Jeremy Benzen suggests.

☐ figure out what your talents are

☐ talk to your parents

☐ get work experience in high school

☐ identify the activities that you like to do

☐ decide what is important to you

A

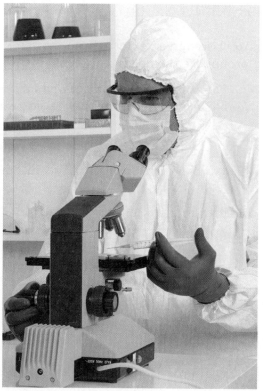

B

2 Look at the pictures. Which shows Jeremy Benzen's job right after college? Which shows the job he has now? Write A or B.

_____ job right after college

_____ job he has now

GO TO MyEnglishLab FOR MORE VOCABULARY PRACTICE.

LISTENING SKILL

1 🎧 Listen to an excerpt from the speech "Finding Your Passion." How does the speaker pronounce the boldfaced words?

*. . . but after a while, I realized that I didn't **want to** get up in the morning and go to work. I* **had to** *figure out what my real passion was.*

REDUCED SPEECH

English words are often reduced in speech. Speakers leave out some sounds and blend words together.

🎧 Listen to these common reductions:

Examples

Unreduced	Reduced
going to	*gonna*
got to	*gotta*
want to	*wanna*
should have	*shoulda*
could have	*coulda*
have to	*hafta*
What are you . . . ?	*Wadaya . . . ?*
Do you . . . ?	*D'ya . . . ?*

2 🎧 Listen to the conversation. Notice the reduced phrases. Then complete the conversation. Write the unreduced form of each phrase.

A: **(1)** ___What are you___ doing after college?

B: I'm **(2)**_____ look for a job. But there's a problem. I'm a business major, but I **(3)**_____ be a teacher. I **(4)**_____ gotten a teaching certificate. **(5)**_____ think I could get a teaching job?

A: I think you should try. There's no rule that says you **(6)**_____ get a job that matches your major.

B: You're right, I've **(7)**_____ think about this some more.

━━━ GO TO MyEnglishLab *FOR MORE SKILL PRACTICE.*

STEP 1: Organize

🎧 Listen to Listenings One and Two again. Then complete the chart with details about career decisions.

	LISTENING ONE: Changing Career Paths		LISTENING TWO: Finding Your Passion
	JULIE HESSION	SIMON SINEK	JEREMY BENZEN
How did the speaker realize he / she needed a career change?	• was unhappy with job and lonely in Annapolis	• _____ _____	• _____ _____
What help did the speaker get from his / her parents, if any?	• _____ _____	• ultimately got support from father	
What strategies did the speaker use to change his / her career direction?	• _____ _____	• _____ _____ • told his parents	• _____ _____ • went back to school

STEP 2: Synthesize

Work in groups of three. Discuss the questions. Support your answers with information from Step 1: Organize. Then compare your answers with those of another group.

1. The people in Listening One and Listening Two came to their career change decisions in different ways. Compare the experiences of the three people. How were they similar / different?

2. Which person seems to have the closest relationship with his / her parent(s)? What leads you to think that this relationship is the closest?

3. Which person had the most effective strategies to change the direction of his / her career? Why do you believe these strategies were the most effective?

━━━ GO TO MyEnglishLab TO CHECK WHAT YOU LEARNED.

VOCABULARY

REVIEW

Complete the paragraphs. Use the boldfaced words. You might have to change the form of some of the words.

1. **figure out / bribe / take a chance**

   My parents really wanted me to be an accountant. They tried to
   _____ me by saying, "If you study accounting, we'll pay for college."
   But my passion is fashion design. I had to _____ a way to pay
   for college myself. It was hard, but today I work in New York in the fashion industry.
   Sometimes you have to _____ and do what you love.

2. **process / supportive / tunnel vision**

   I've always wanted to be a doctor, ever since I was a kid. Some people say I
   have _____, but it's the only career I want. I know it's a long
   _____ to become a doctor, with many years of school. Thankfully,
   my family is very _____, so I know I can achieve my goal.

3. **management / strategy / environment**

   I started working in a restaurant after high school. I learned a lot about the restaurant
   business from that job, like how to work in a fast-paced _____ and how
   to give great customer service. Slowly, I moved up into a _____ position.
   I had a simple _____ for getting here: I worked hard and learned as
   much as possible on the job.

4. **major / shift / volunteer**

   When I went to college, I wanted to study business. Then I _____ for an
   afterschool program and helped children with their homework. After that experience,
   my career goal _____ away from business. I decided to change my
   _____ to education, and today I'm a teacher.

5. enroll / drop out / ultimately

I started studying to be a pharmacist, but I didn't like it. I _____ of school and worked in a clothing store for a few years. Then I _____ in a new school and studied computer programming. I _____ graduated last year, and now I have a great job in software development.

EXPAND

1 Read the tips. Notice the boldfaced words.

Tips for New Employees

Congratulations! You are starting a new job. Here are some tips to help you **(1) play your cards right** and succeed in your new position.

Listen and learn
As a new employee, you should watch and listen. Don't try to give your opinion on every issue. Be ready to **(2) play second fiddle** to more experienced co-workers. With time, you can take more of a leadership role.

Ask questions
Make sure you understand your work assignments. If not, talk to your boss or co-workers and **(3) get the lowdown**. Get the information you need to complete your assignments effectively.

Be helpful
Look for things that need to be done, even if they aren't part of your job description: Copy and staple a report for a meeting? Clean up the break room? Show your co-workers that you are willing to **(4) get your hands dirty**.

Be flexible
Be ready to **(5) play it by ear**. Surprises happen, and you should know how to respond to unexpected situations.

Ask for help
You are new in your job, so you still have a lot to learn. Don't hide your problems or mistakes. Ask for help immediately and don't wait for problems to **(6) get out of hand**.

---

2 Match the boldfaced words with the meanings. Write the correct number.

_____ **a.** to accept that you have a lower position

_____ **b.** to act without preparation

_____ **c.** to become involved in all aspects of something, including work that is unpleasant or less interesting

_____ **d.** to become uncontrolled

_____ **e.** to do everything necessary to succeed

_____ **f.** to get the facts about something

(1) play your cards right

(2) play second fiddle

(3) get the lowdown

(4) get your hands dirty

(5) play it by ear

(6) get out of hand

CREATE

Work with a partner. Take turns giving and getting career advice. Follow the steps.

1. Ask your partner the questions.

   - What is your career goal? (If you are unsure, think about one or two careers that you might enjoy.)

   - What are the difficulties that might prevent you from reaching that goal?

2. Give your partner advice about his or her career. Use expressions from the list.

Possible Advice

- **drop out** of a class and **enroll** in a new class

- **shift** your career in a new direction

- **take a chance**

- **volunteer** somewhere

- **figure out** a **strategy**

- **major** in _____

- have **tunnel vision**

- talk to a **supportive** family member / friend

- go through a **process** to find your passion

- **get the lowdown** on new jobs in your city

- **play your cards right** and follow up on opportunities

GO TO MyEnglishLab FOR MORE VOCABULARY PRACTICE.

GRAMMAR

1 Read the excerpt from a book about how to find a job. Underline the **infinitive verbs** (**to** + base form).

> Here are a few hints to help you find the job of your dreams:
>
> **1)** Do research <u>to discover</u> what jobs are available.
>
> **2)** Apply for interesting jobs early in order to get a good interview time.
>
> **3)** Get to your job interview early in order to make a good impression.
>
> **4)** After the interview, send the interviewer a thank you note to remind him / her of your conversation.

INFINITIVES OF PURPOSE

1. Use an **infinitive of purpose** to explain the purpose of an action.	
• Use *to* + **base form**.	*I did some Internet research **to get** an idea of the kinds of jobs I might like.*
• Use *in order to* + **base form**.	*I read my résumé carefully **in order to find** grammatical mistakes.*
It often answers the question *Why?*	A: *Why did Gina quit her job?*
	B: *She quit her job **to follow** her passion.*
2. *To* + **base form** is more common in informal speech.	*I took a personality test **to see** what jobs would be a good match for me.*
In order to + **base form** is more common in formal speech and writing.	*I took a personality test **in order to see** what jobs would be a good match for me.*
3. Use *in order not to* to explain a negative purpose.	*I set my alarm clock early **in order not to miss** my job interview.*
In informal speech, you can also use *because* + **a reason** to express a negative purpose.	*I set my alarm clock early **because I didn't want to miss** my job interview.*

2 Work with a partner. Rewrite each sentence using an infinitive of purpose.

1. Julie went to college because she wanted to study hotel management.

   Julie went to college in order to study hotel management.

2. Julie moved to Annapolis, Maryland, because she wanted to begin her first job working in a hotel.

(continued on next page)

3. Julie didn't complain about her job because she didn't want to disappoint her parents.

_____

4. Julie's dad took her to lunch because he wanted to talk with her about her job.

_____

5. After college Simon went to law school because he wanted to become a lawyer.

_____

6. Simon's parents tried everything because they wanted to stop Simon from dropping out of law school.

_____

7. Simon dropped out of law school because he wanted to study marketing.

_____

3 With your partner, take turns giving each other job search advice. Use an idea from the list + an infinitive of purpose and / or reason. Listen to your partner and help him / her correct any errors.

Example

STUDENT 1:   Before you look for a job, talk with a job counselor to help you identify your skills.

a. talk with a job counselor

b. go to a job fair

c. volunteer

d. make a list of things that are important

e. get a friend to read your résumé

f. wear nice clothes to an interview

g. ask friends and family for advice

h. follow your passion in life

GO TO MyEnglishLab FOR MORE GRAMMAR PRACTICE.

PRONUNCIATION

INTONATION FOR *YES/NO* AND *WH-* QUESTIONS

Intonation is the pattern of high and low notes in language. When we ask a question, our voice gets higher or lower, depending on the kind of question.

🎧 Listen to and read the conversation between two friends. At the end of each question, notice how the speaker's voice gets higher (rising intonation) or lower (falling intonation).

Example

MARY:	I heard you got a new job. **Do you like it?**
JOHN:	It's great. I love teaching!
MARY:	**What grade are you teaching?**
JOHN:	First grade. They're a fun class!

Yes / no **questions** end with rising intonation. Your voice gets higher at the end of the question.	*Are you a teacher?* *Do you have a big class?*
Wh- **questions** end with falling intonation. Your voice gets lower at the end of the question.	*Why did you decide to become a teacher?* *How long have you been teaching?*

1   🎧 Listen to John's job interview. Mark the correct intonation at the end of each question. Use arrows [↘] or [↗].

PRINCIPAL:	**(1)** How long have you been teaching? _____
JOHN:	I've been teaching for five years.
PRINCIPAL:	**(2)** Have you ever taught first grade? _____
JOHN:	No, but I've taught second grade, so I know what skills students in first grade need in order to move on.
PRINCIPAL:	Good point! **(3)** How do you feel about teaching younger children? _____
JOHN:	I'd love to teach younger children. First grade is a big year because many children start reading.
PRINCIPAL:	Yes, it *is* an important year. **(4)** Are you familiar with our reading program? _____
JOHN:	I am. I used a similar program at my last school.

2 Compare your answers with a partner's. Then role-play the job interview. Then switch roles.

3 Work with a new partner. Student 1 is applying for a teaching job. Student 2 is the school office manager. The office manager needs to complete the New Teacher Information form by asking the teacher **yes / no** and **wh-** questions. Pay attention to rising and falling question intonation. Switch roles and repeat the activity.

New Teacher Information

Name: _____ _____ _____
          (first)   (middle)   (surname)

Address: _____

Phone: _____

Emergency contact person: _____
                              (name)

Emergency contact person: _____
                              (phone)

Medical problems? Yes _____ No _____

   If yes, list problems: _____

   _____

   _____

Need parking space? Yes _____ No _____

Paycheck sent directly to bank? Yes _____ No _____

   If no, check will be delivered at school.

SPEAKING SKILL

ASKING FOLLOW-UP QUESTIONS

A **follow-up question** is a question that comes from the answer to a previous question.

🎧 Read and listen to the conversation. When Robert hears Jane say that she isn't doing well, he asks a follow-up question to find out what is wrong.

Example

ROBERT:	Hi Jane. How are you?
JANE:	Not so good.
ROBERT:	What's wrong?

Three main purposes of follow-up questions:	
• to show that you are listening	*Really?*
• to ask for clarification (to ask the speaker to repeat or explain because you don't understand)	*Did you say he's difficult?*
• to get more information	*What does he do that makes him difficult?*

To ask a follow-up question:		
• listen carefully to the speaker	JANE:	*He's so **difficult** to work with.*
	ROBERT:	*Did you say he's **difficult**?*
• choose a word / phrase or an idea from the speaker and ask a question about it	JANE:	*Yes.*
	ROBERT:	*What does he do that makes him **difficult**?*

---

1 Work with a partner. Complete the conversation with follow-up questions. Then practice the conversation. Switch roles and repeat.

ROBERT:	Hi Jane. How are you?
JANE:	Not so good.
ROBERT:	**(1)** _____ What's wrong?
JANE:	I really don't like my new boss.
ROBERT:	Why?
JANE:	Well, for one thing, he's very strict about getting to work on time.
ROBERT:	What time **(2)** _____?
JANE:	Well, I'm supposed to arrive at 8:00, but sometimes I might be five minutes late.

(continued on next page)

ROBERT: What happens if (3) _____?

JANE: He gets really angry and starts yelling at me.

ROBERT: Did you say (4) _____?

JANE: Yes, he yells so loud that all the other employees can hear.

ROBERT: That must be embarrassing! Does he (5) _____?

JANE: Yes, he does it to everyone.

2 Work in groups of four. Student A finishes one of the statements with personal information. The other students take turns asking follow-up questions. Student A answers. Repeat the activity until each student has made two personal statements.

Example

Yesterday I _____.

A: Yesterday I saw a great movie!

B: Oh, really?

A: Yes, really!

C: What movie did you see?

A: *Batman.*

D: What was great about it?

A: It had lots of action and great special effects.

Statements

Today I'm going to _____.	I wish I could _____.
I need to _____.	In my opinion _____.
I really like _____.	I'm trying to figure out _____.
Next year I'm planning to _____.	My dream job is _____.

■■■■■■■■■■■■■■■■■■■■■■■■■■ GO TO MyEnglishLab *FOR MORE SKILL PRACTICE AND TO CHECK WHAT YOU LEARNED.*

FINAL SPEAKING TASK

A job interview is a formal conversation between an employer and a job candidate (a person who has applied for a job). The employer asks questions about the candidate's education, work history, and job skills. The candidate answers the questions and tries to show why he / she is the best person for the job.

In this activity, you will create and perform a job interview role play.

Follow the steps. Try to use the vocabulary, grammar, pronunciation, and listening and speaking skills that you learned in this unit.*

STEP 1: Imagine that you have an interview for your dream job. Choose a job that you want from the list below, or think of another job. Then think of a company you want to work for.

Job Titles

accountant	doctor	librarian
bank teller	engineer	nurse
computer programmer	firefighter	teacher
cook	lawyer	television producer

STEP 2: Think about the reasons that an employer should hire you. On a separate piece of paper, write the job title and answer the questions below. Take notes, listing three things for each question and include an example with each.

Job Title:

1. What am I good at?

2. What do I like to do?

3. What is important to me?

Example

Job Title: _Nurse at Memorial Hospital_

1. What am I good at?

_____science_____ **Example:** _enjoy lab work_

2. What do I like to do?

helping people **Example:** _Red Cross volunteer_

3. What is important to me in a job?

working with people **Example:** _not being alone in a lab_

---

*For Alternative Speaking Topics, see page 127.

STEP 3: Work with a partner. Role-play a job interview. Take turns being the employer and the job candidate.

Employer: Ask the candidate which job he / she is applying for. Interview the candidate to find out if he / she is the best person for the job. Ask the job interview questions below, and add one question of your own.[1] Ask follow-up questions to get more information.

Interview Questions

1. Tell me about your education and work experience.

2. Why are you interested in this job?

3. What are your greatest strengths?

4. How does this job fit with your future career plans?

5. Your question: _____

Job Candidate: Answer the employer's questions using the ideas from your notes in Step 2. Give specific details and examples to show why you are the best person for the job.

STEP 4: Switch partners and repeat the role play.

Listening Task

As you interview the candidate, rate his or her answers from 1 (Poor) to 5 (Good). A good answer a) answers the question you asked, b) is clear and easy to understand, and c) includes details and examples.

Name: _____					
Job Title: _____					
	Poor				Good
Question 1	1	2	3	4	5
Question 2	1	2	3	4	5
Question 3	1	2	3	4	5
Question 4	1	2	3	4	5
Question 5	1	2	3	4	5
Overall interview	1	2	3	4	5

---

[1] In the United States, it is illegal for employers to ask personal questions about age, ethnicity, marriage status, number of children, or religion. This is to prevent discrimination against job candidates for these reasons.

UNIT PROJECT

STEP 1: Find a person who has an unusual or interesting career.

STEP 2: Interview this person about his / her current job. Use the questions to guide your interview and add your own questions. Take notes during the interview.

1. What is your job? Can you describe what you do?

2. What do you like about your job? What don't you like?

3. How did you become a _____? Please explain the steps that you went through after high school to get your job.

4. Would you like to continue with your career? Why or why not?

5. _____

STEP 3: Do online research to find interesting statistics or background information about the job or to answer any remaining questions.

STEP 4: Use your notes to write a summary of the interview. Read your summary to the class. Talk about one idea from the interview that you thought was interesting or important.

ALTERNATIVE SPEAKING TOPICS

Read the quotes about careers. Do you agree with them? Why or why not? Share your thoughts with the class.

1. Quote: "No man can succeed in a line of endeavor which he does not like."
   —Napoleon Hill, writer
   Paraphrase: People cannot succeed in jobs they don't like.

2. Quote: "I think everyone should experience defeat at least once during their career. You learn a lot from it."
   —Lou Holtz, coach, writer, speaker
   Paraphrase: Everyone should fail at least once in a career. You can learn a lot from failure.

3. Quote: "Each man has his own vocation; his talent is his call. There is one direction in which all space is open for him."
   —Ralph Waldo Emerson, writer
   Paraphrase: Everyone has a talent. There is one direction that is open for you to follow in life and that is the direction your talent takes you.

■■■■■■■■■■■■■■■■■■■■■■■■■■■■■■■■ GO TO MyEnglishLab TO DISCUSS ONE OF THE ALTERNATIVE TOPICS, WATCH A VIDEO ABOUT CAREERS, AND TAKE THE UNIT 5 ACHIEVEMENT TEST. ■■■■■■■■■■■■■■■■■■■■■■

CULTURE AND
Commerce

1. Look at the photo. Why do you think these women are wearing coils around their necks?

2. Read the title of the unit. *Commerce* means business. In your opinion, what is the relationship between culture and commerce in tourism?

3. In what ways can tourism be helpful in a community? In what ways can it be harmful?

GO TO MyEnglishLab TO CHECK WHAT YOU KNOW.

2 FOCUS ON LISTENING

VOCABULARY

1 🎧 A travel blog is an Internet site where people write about their trips. Read and listen to the travel blog about a trip to Thailand. Notice the boldfaced words.

TRAVEL BLOG: NORTHERN THAILAND

HOME

CONTACT

ABOUT ME

We've had a great time exploring Northern Thailand so far. It's really interesting, and there's so much to see!

One thing I've learned is that elephants are the national symbol of Thailand. They're very important in Thai history and cultural **(a) traditions**. Elephants are also a big **(b) tourist attraction**, so there are many different elephant parks for tourists to visit. We decided to visit one, but we soon found out that there's a lot of **(c) controversy** about them. Some parks treat the elephants very badly. They're not treated with respect and have to

perform **(d) degrading** tricks for tourists, like playing basketball and dancing. The owners don't really care about the elephants; they just want to **(e) make a living** by showing the animals to tourists.

However, the elephant park we went to is very different. In this place, they're trying to **(f) preserve** the wild elephant population. It's a large, beautiful park where the elephants can walk around freely. They are so playful! I took this photo of two young elephants walking together with their trunks **(g) wrapped** around each other, just like two kids walking hand-in-hand. Going to the park was an amazing experience, much better than seeing elephants in a **(h) zoo**. I also bought some nice **(i) souvenirs**: a stuffed elephant toy for my niece and a carved wooden elephant for my parents.

Tomorrow we're going to see another unusual sight: the village of Nai Soi where the long-necked women of the Padaung tribe live. The women wear brass coils to **(j) stretch** their necks. More on that tomorrow!

2 Match the boldfaced words from the reading to the definitions. Write the correct letter.

_____ **1.** a disagreement among people

_____ **2.** a place where animals are kept so that people can look at them

_____ **3.** to keep something from being changed or harmed

_____ **4.** customs (special activities) that have existed for a long time

_____ **5.** things you buy to help you remember a place

_____ **6.** to make something longer by pulling it

_____ **7.** folded around something

_____ **8.** showing no respect

_____ **9.** something interesting for a tourist to see or do

_____ **10.** to earn money from

GO TO MyEnglishLab FOR MORE VOCABULARY PRACTICE.

PREVIEW

A journalist reports on the long-necked women of Padaung and the tourists who travel to Nai Soi to see them.

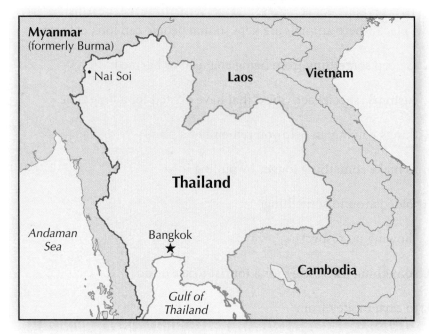

🎧 Listen to an excerpt from the report. Circle your prediction.

This news report will present the tourist attraction in _____.

a. a positive way

b. a negative way

c. a way that is both positive and negative

MAIN IDEAS

1 🎧 Listen to the whole report. Look again at your prediction from the Preview section. How did your prediction help you understand the report?

2 Read the statements. Write **T** (true) or **F** (false).

The tradition of the long-necked women . . .

_____ **1.** started in Thailand.

_____ **2.** brings tourists to the village to buy souvenirs and take pictures.

_____ **3.** allows women to earn money for their families.

_____ **4.** makes women's necks stronger.

_____ **5.** has caused controversy among tourists.

_____ **6.** will continue as long as tourists keep coming.

DETAILS

Listen again. Complete each statement. Circle the correct answer.

1. About _____ tourists visit the long-necked women every year.

    a. 1,000

    b. 10,000

    c. 100,000

2. When they lived in Myanmar, the Padaung _____.

    a. sold souvenirs to tourists

    b. fought in a war

    c. were farmers

3. A full set of brass coils _____.

    a. weighs up to 22 pounds

    b. costs up to $22

    c. takes up to 22 years to put on

4. A long-necked woman cannot remove the coils because _____.

    a. her neck is very weak

    b. they are made of brass

    c. her family won't let her

5. Back in Myanmar, the tradition of stretching women's necks _____.

    a. has almost disappeared

    b. is still strong

    c. is becoming more popular

(continued on next page)

6. A long-necked woman can make $70 to $80 _____ from tourists.

    a. a week

    b. a month

    c. a year

7. Sandra feels that she is helping the Padaung women because she is _____.

    a. spending money in the village

    b. not visiting the village

    c. bringing medicine to the village

8. Fredrick uses the image of _____ to describe the Padaung women.

    a. animals in a zoo

    b. prisoners in jail

    c. actors in a show

GO TO MyEnglishLab FOR MORE LISTENING PRACTICE.

MAKE INFERENCES

INFERRING EMOTION FROM WORD CHOICE

A speaker may use certain words to express his or her feelings indirectly. The listener can infer the speaker's emotions by paying attention to word choice.

Example

The brass coils are beautiful.
We can infer from the word *beautiful* that the speaker has positive feelings about the brass coils.

The brass coils are painful.
We can infer from the word *painful* that the speaker has negative feelings about the brass coils.

The brass coils are made in the village.
The phrase *made in the village* is not positive or negative. It is neutral. The speaker is not expressing emotion.

🎧 Read and listen to the example. Does Sandra feel positive, negative, or neutral about spending money in Nai Soi?

Example

SANDRA: *. . . and so if I go, it's like I'm helping them to preserve it. Spending my money is also helping them. You know, they make a living from tourism, so they need us.*

Sandra's feelings about spending money in Nai Soi are positive. She uses words such as *preserve* and *helping*, which have a positive meaning, so we can infer that she has positive feelings.

1 🎧 Listen to excerpts from the report and focus on the speaker's word choice. How does the speaker feel? Read each statement. Circle the correct answer.

Excerpt One

The reporter's feelings about the Padaung's new lives in Nai Soi are _____.

a. positive

b. negative

c. neutral

Excerpt Two

Fredrick's feelings about the tradition of neck stretching are _____.

a. positive

b. negative

c. neutral

2 Work with a partner. Talk about the information that helped you find the answers.

EXPRESS OPINIONS

Work in a small group. Discuss the statements. Do you agree or disagree? Explain your opinions.

1. I would like to visit the women of the Padaung tribe.

2. The Padaung women are helped by the tourism in their village.

============================== GO TO MyEnglishLab TO GIVE YOUR OPINION ABOUT ANOTHER QUESTION.

LISTENING TWO TOWN HALL MEETING IN CAPE COD

VOCABULARY

1 Read the information about Cape Cod. Notice the boldfaced words. What can you conclude about this tourist destination?

Cape Cod, Massachusetts

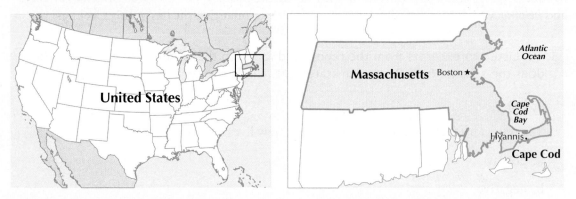

Cape Cod is one of New England's most popular tourist attractions. Tourism has **developed** quickly, and now the area is visited by more than 5 million tourists each year. During the summer **season**, from June to September, tourists come to relax at the beach, shop in the small towns, and eat fresh seafood. During the rest of the year, the population drops to about 200,000, and Cape Cod becomes a small **community** again. Many summer businesses, such as restaurants and souvenir shops, close for the winter because they cannot **afford** to pay their workers' **salaries** once the tourists leave.

2 Match the boldfaced words with the definitions. Write the correct letter.

__e__   **1. develop**   **a.** to have enough money to pay for something

_____   **2. season**   **b.** one of the four main periods (times) in the year

_____   **3. community**   **c.** a group of people who live in the same town

_____   **4. afford**   **d.** money that workers receive regularly as payment for their work

_____   **5. salary**

                         ~~**e.** to grow into something bigger~~

COMPREHENSION

Listen to a town hall meeting. The mayor (the town leader) is leading the meeting. The townspeople are listening and expressing their opinions. Complete each statement. Circle the correct answer.

1. The traffic on Cape Cod _____.

     a. gets worse during the summer

     b. is bad all year

     c. is better now that there are buses

2. _____ is difficult to find on Cape Cod.

     a. Housing for regular people

     b. Housing near shops and restaurants

     c. Vacation housing

3. The restaurant owner knows a waitress who lives _____.

     a. in her car

     b. far from her work

     c. in a hotel

(continued on next page)

4. The woman who runs the souvenir shop says _____.

    a. she plans to open another store next year in a neighboring village

    b. she does most of her business during the summer

    c. her business is doing badly this year

5. The male business owner says he lost money because _____.

    a. too many stores are selling the same things

    b. tourists go to the beach instead of going shopping

    c. the rainy weather kept tourists away

■■■■■■■■■■■■■■■■■■■■■■■■■■■■■■■■■■■■ *GO TO* MyEnglishLab *FOR MORE VOCABULARY PRACTICE.*

LISTENING SKILL

1 🎧 Listen to an excerpt from the town hall meeting. What words does the speaker use to show that he is going to state an opinion?

LISTENING FOR OPINIONS

Expressions to Signal an Opinion

It is useful to know when a person is going to state an opinion. Speakers use many different expressions to introduce opinions. For example:

. . . in my opinion   *. . . I think that*   *. . . I believe*

🎧 Read and listen to the example. Notice the signal words.

Example

    *I agree, traffic gets bad, but **in my mind** the biggest problem is housing.*

The speaker uses the phrase "in my mind" to signal that he is going to state an opinion. His opinion is that housing is the biggest problem caused by tourists.

2 🎧 Listen to the excerpts. Complete each statement. Write the expression that signals an opinion. Then write the speaker's opinion.

Excerpt One

        WOMAN 2:   OK, I know it's difficult to have all these tourists around during the summer, but _____ am . . .

SPEAKER'S OPINION: _____

> MAN 2:   But I'm a business owner too, and one problem _____
>   is that . . .

SPEAKER'S OPINION: _____

> MAN 2:   _____ us develop where we . . .

SPEAKER'S OPINION: _____

▪▪▪▪▪▪▪▪▪▪▪▪▪▪▪▪▪▪▪▪▪▪▪▪▪▪▪▪▪▪▪▪▪▪▪▪▪▪ GO TO MyEnglishLab FOR MORE SKILL PRACTICE.

CONNECT THE LISTENINGS

STEP 1: Organize

1 🎧 Listen to Listenings One and Two again. Then complete the chart with details about the effects of tourism.

	POSITIVE EFFECTS OF TOURISM	NEGATIVE EFFECTS OF TOURISM
LISTENING ONE: PADAUNG TRIBE	1. _____ 2. Tourism is easier than farming. 3. _____	1. Women continue to wrap their necks. 2. _____
LISTENING TWO: CAPE COD RESIDENTS	1. _____	1. Traffic gets bad. 2. _____ 3. _____

2 Draw a circle around the effect that is similar in both communities.

STEP 2: Synthesize

Work with a partner. Debate the topic "Does tourism help or hurt people in tourist communities?" One person takes the pro position (Tourism has positive effects on people in tourist communities). The other person takes the con position (Tourism has negative effects on people in tourist communities). Each person has 2–3 minutes to present his or her position. Use the information from Step 1: Organize to support your position.

Then switch partners and repeat the debate two more times with new partners.

▪▪▪▪▪▪▪▪▪▪▪▪▪▪▪▪▪▪▪▪▪▪▪▪▪▪▪▪▪▪▪▪▪▪▪▪▪▪ GO TO MyEnglishLab TO CHECK WHAT YOU LEARNED.

VOCABULARY

Cross out the word that doesn't belong in each group. Consult a dictionary if necessary.

1. zoo — ~~museum~~ — animal park — wildlife center

2. afford — have money for — pay for — borrow from

3. controversy — argument — debate — agreement

4. degrading — polite — embarrassing — painful

5. make a living — earn a salary — enjoy life — get paid

6. preserve — develop — save — care for

7. season — days of the week — time of year — period of time

8. souvenir — reminder — keepsake — equipment

9. tourist attraction — place to see — guidebook — point of interest

10. tradition — habit — change — belief

11. community — small town — village — city

1 Read the letter to the editor about the effects of tourism in Cape Cod. Notice the boldfaced words.

TO THE EDITOR

Effects of Tourism

Millions of tourists visit Cape Cod each year. Most tourists come here to relax at the beach and enjoy our delicious seafood. Others like to **get off the beaten path** and explore parts of the Cape that most tourists don't see. Whatever they do here, we appreciate the tourists because most **locals** have jobs that depend on tourism, such as shop owners and restaurants workers.

However, tourism can also **have a** negative **impact** on the area. The cost of housing is one example. The cost of housing keeps increasing, so many families can't afford to buy a home. **In the long run**, this problem will force families to leave the Cape and live elsewhere.

Problems like this affect our **way of life** here on the Cape. Life is becoming more difficult for the year-round residents. We need to **find a compromise** that will preserve the tourist income for the area and allow the locals to continue living here.

Michelle Connelly
Sandwich, Mass.

2 Match the words with the definitions. Write the correct letter.

_____ **1.** get off the beaten path
a. to have an effect on someone or something

_____ **2.** locals
b. customs and habits of daily living

_____ **3.** have an impact
c. far in the future

_____ **4.** in the long run
d. to go somewhere that most tourists don't visit

_____ **5.** way of life
e. to look for ideas that opposing groups can agree on

_____ **6.** find a compromise
f. people who live in a place year around

CREATE

Work in a small group. Each person thinks of a tourist destination he or she has visited. Take turns making a short presentation about the destination. Answer the questions. Use the vocabulary from the box.

Questions

1. What tourist destination did you visit?

2. What are the major tourist attractions?

3. What impact does tourism have on the locals?

4. What impact does tourism have on the environment?

afford	get off the beaten path	preserve
controversial	in the long run	season
degrading	locals	souvenir
find a compromise	make a living	way of life

GO TO MyEnglishLab *FOR MORE VOCABULARY PRACTICE.*

GRAMMAR

1 Work with a partner. Read the conversation between two residents of Cape Cod. Then switch roles and repeat. Notice the boldfaced **predictions**.

A: Did you see the weather report today? They say it**'ll keep** raining all week.

B: Really? That's bad. If **it keeps** raining, the tourists **won't come**. They**'ll stay** home.

A: I know. I**'ll probably lose** money this week.

PREDICTIONS WITH *WILL* AND *IF*-CLAUSES

1. Use *will* and *will not (won't)* to make predictions. *Will* is usually contracted in speech.	*It **will rain** again next week.* *Tourists **won't come** to the shops and restaurants.* *They**'ll stay** home.*
2. Use *probably* with *will* to show less certainty.	*Business **will probably be** slow all week.* *I **probably won't make** enough money.*
3. Use *if*-clauses to talk about possible results in the future.	[*if*-clause]　　　　　　　　[main clause] *If the rain **continues**, we**'ll have** a lot of problems.* [main clause]　　　　　　　　[*if*-clause] *We**'ll have** a lot of problems if the rain **continues**.*

2 Complete the paragraphs. Use the words in parentheses. Use contractions of **will** where possible.

1. If it _____ rains _____ a lot this summer, fewer tourists _____ will visit _____.
   　　　　　　(rain)　　　　　　　　　　　　　　　　　　　　　　(visit)
   Businesses _____ probably won't make _____ enough money. Some shops
   　　　　　　　(probably / not / make)
   _____ will probably close _____.
   　　　　(probably / close)

2. If housing _____ more expensive, many families
   　　　　　　　　　　　(get)
   _____ afford a house on Cape Cod. Some families,
   　　(not / be able to)
   _____ and others _____ renting.
   　(probably / move away)　　　　　　　　　　　(continue)

3. I heard that another seafood restaurant _____ in town. If it
   　　　　　　　　　　　　　　　　　　　　(probably / open)
   _____, there _____ more jobs for the
   　　　(open)　　　　　　　　　　　　　　　(be)
   locals. But the other restaurants in town _____ customers.
   　　　　　　　　　　　　　　　　　　　　(probably / lose)

4. Traffic _____ worse if more tourists
   　　　　　　　(get)
   _____ their cars to Cape Cod. There
   　　　(bring)
   _____ enough parking spaces at the beach.
   　(probably / not / be)

3 Work with a partner. Read about the people who live and vacation on Cape Cod. Take turns asking about the future and making predictions. What will happen to these people if tourism increases on Cape Cod? What will happen if tourism decreases?

Example

STUDENT A: What **will happen** to Joe if tourism increases?

STUDENT B: If tourism **increases**, Joe's restaurant **will probably get** busier.

STUDENT A: I agree. He**'ll serve** more seafood every day. He**'ll probably need** to hire more cooks and waitresses. . . .

CAPE COD PORTRAITS

Joe . . .

- owns Joe's Seafood Shack.
- serves 100 pounds of seafood each day.
- employs five cooks and four waitresses.

Bill and Maureen . . .

- own the Cape Art Gallery.
- sell paintings and jewelry from local artists.
- employ two salesclerks.

Sandy . . .

- is a high school student.
- works in a local souvenir shop during the summer.
- saves money to go to college.

The Harvey family . . .

- vacations on Cape Cod every summer.
- rents a house from a local.
- enjoys the area because the beaches aren't crowded.

GO TO MyEnglishLab FOR MORE GRAMMAR PRACTICE.

PRONUNCIATION

SOME PRONUNCIATION AND SPELLING RULES FOR *O*

The letter *o* has many different pronunciations in English. In the words *hotel, shop, come, woman,* and *move,* the letter *o* has five different pronunciations. Sometimes the letters around *o* can help you guess how to pronounce the vowel, but not always.

🎧 Read and listen to the example. Notice how the letter **o** is pronounced. Is it pronounced the same in any of the words?

Example

*The **long**-necked **women** of Padaung talk with tourists, **pose** for pictures, and sell souvenirs. They have **become** an important source of **commerce** and **money** in small villages **along** the Thai / Myanmar border.*

	Spelling	Pronunciation Tips
a)	*o* + a consonant + silent *e* *home, bone, pose, hope, close*	🎧 /ow/, like the vowel in *go*. Keep rounding your lips.
b)	*o* + one or more consonants *shop, lot, job, commerce, problem*	🎧 /a/, like the vowel in *father*; this vowel has no "o" sound. Do not round your lips.
c)	*o* + *ng, ss, st, ll, ff* *long, boss, lost, collar, office*	🎧 /ɔ/, like the vowel in *law*. This vowel is like /a/, but the lips are a little rounded. NOTE: Some Americans pronounce these words with /a/, like the vowel in *father*. You can use this vowel, too.
	Exceptions	**Pronunciation Tips**
d)	*come, mother, brother, love, other*	🎧 /ə/, like the vowel in *cut*. Your mouth is almost closed.
e)	*move, lose*	🎧 /uw/, like the vowel in *do*
f)	*woman*	🎧 /u/, like the vowel in *could*
g)	*women*	🎧 /ɪ/, like the vowel in *sit*

1 🎧 Listen to the words and repeat them.

1. positive	7. won't	13. controversy
2. progress	8. money	14. sold
3. economic	9. vote	15. option
4. modern	10. popular	16. hospital
5. proposal	11. company	17. ocean
6. month	12. local	18. done

2 Work with a partner. How is the letter **o** pronounced in the words in Exercise 1? Complete the chart. The number in parentheses tells you how many words are in that column. Ask your teacher to repeat the words if you're not sure. Compare your answers with the class's.

O SOUNDS LIKE . . .		
THE VOWEL IN *FATHER* (8)	THE VOWEL IN *GO* (6)	THE VOWEL IN *CUT* (4)
positive		

3 Make phrases by writing words from the box in the blanks. Check your answers with a partner's. Practice saying the phrases to your partner. Pronounce the vowels carefully.

economic	local	modern	popular	positive

1. _____economic_____ progress (business, jobs)

2. _____ controversy (not in earlier times)

3. _____ proposal (one that will have good results)

4. _____ option (one people like)

5. _____ company (in this area)

SPEAKING SKILL

MAKING SUGGESTIONS

When you make a suggestion, you give ideas about what you think someone should do. Suggestions can be *stronger* when you strongly believe the other person should follow your advice or *weaker* when you don't feel as strongly.

Stronger	*We should (definitely) . . .*	*visit an elephant park.*
	We (definitely) shouldn't . . .	
	Let's (not) . . .	
	I think / don't think we should . . .	
Weaker	*One option is to . . .*	*visit an elephant park.*
	We might (not) want to . . .	
	We could . . .	
	Why don't we . . .	
	What do you think of . . .	*visiting an elephant park?*
	How about . . .	

1 🎧 Work with a partner. Read and listen to the conversation between two tourists in Thailand. Notice the suggestions in bold. Which are stronger? Which are weaker?

A: What do you want to do tomorrow? **One option is to** visit an elephant park.

B: That's a great idea! Then **we could** go to Padaung to see the long-necked women.

A: **Let's not** go there. I think it's degrading for the women.

B: OK, but **we definitely shouldn't** miss the elephant park.

2 Read each pair of suggestions with your partner. Circle the one that is stronger. Discuss the difference between the two suggestions.

1. **a.** Let's take a guided tour.

   b. How about taking a guided tour?

2. **a.** We might want to buy souvenirs.

   b. We should definitely buy souvenirs.

3. **a.** I think we should eat at the hotel.

   b. One option is to eat at the hotel.

(continued on next page)

4. a. We could go to the elephant park today.

  b. Let's not go to the elephant park today.

5. a. What do you think of visiting the long-necked women?

  b. I don't think we should visit the long-necked women.

3 Imagine that you are going to spend four days in Bangkok, Thailand. What would you like to do? Read the list of activity choices and take turns making suggestions with your partner.

ACTIVITY CHOICES

Animals

- Go to Dusit Zoo to see wild animals.
- Visit the Snake Farm and see venom[1] removed from snakes to make medicine.
- Volunteer at an elephant park and help take care of the elephants.

Shopping

- Buy books about Thailand from Asia Books.
- Find fashionable women's clothing at Siam Square shops.
- Go to Lao Song Handicrafts to buy traditional Thai crafts and souvenirs.

Sightseeing

- Go to the National Museum and learn about Thai art.
- Visit the Grand Palace to see where Thai kings lived.
- Go to the Wat Sai floating market, where farmers sell food on boats.

Off the Beaten Path

- Spend a day at a spa, enjoying a massage, skin care, and a sauna.
- Take a Thai cooking class at the Blue Elephant Cooking School.
- Go on a bike tour of Bangkok.

■■■■■■■■■■■■■■■■■■■■■■■■■■ GO TO MyEnglishLab FOR MORE SKILL PRACTICE AND TO CHECK WHAT YOU LEARNED.

---

[1] **venom:** poisonous liquid that snakes produce

FINAL SPEAKING TASK

A simulation is an activity that reflects a real-life situation.

In this activity, you will participate in a simulation about the effects of tourism. You will talk about a controversial proposal to build a hotel in a rainforest. You will need to negotiate your ideas and reach a compromise.

Work in a group. Read the situation about a company that wants to build a hotel. Then follow the steps. Try to use the vocabulary, grammar, pronunciation, and listening and speaking skills that you learned in this unit.*

SITUATION

Royal Hotels wants to build a large 300-room resort hotel on Coral Beach, a quiet beach next to a small fishing village. Coral Beach has only a few tourists now, but the company has studied the area and thinks it can be a popular tourist attraction. Tourists can:

- enjoy the beautiful beaches
- visit the local fishing village
- explore the nearby rainforest

The proposal is controversial. In order to build the resort, Royal Hotels would need to build a road through the rainforest. The rainforest is a protected area that is managed by Landwatch, an environmental group. Landwatch is worried about the impact the hotel will have on the environment and wildlife. In addition, local residents in the fishing village are worried about the negative impact on their way of life.

*For Alternative Speaking Tasks, see page 153.

STEP 1: Work in three groups. Group A takes the position of representatives of Royal Hotels, Group B takes the position of the Landwatch group, and Group C takes the position of the local villagers. Read your group's position below and on page 151. **Do not read other groups' positions.** Talk about the positive and negative impacts of the hotel. Take notes.

Group A: Royal Hotels

Your group represents the needs and wants of tourists visiting the area.

- In order to build the hotel, Royal Hotels needs permission from Landwatch to build a road through the rainforest.

- The hotel needs workers in the hotel (restaurants, shops, etc.) and to run tourist services such as area and fishing tours.

- In a hotel survey, tourists said they want to:
  - visit natural areas like the ocean and the jungle, and see wildlife
  - go to nice, clean beaches
  - eat at good restaurants
  - see life in a traditional fishing village
  - go sport fishing

- Royal Hotels is willing to give $1 million to preserve natural areas and / or help the fishing village.

Group B: Landwatch

Your group represents the needs of the environment: the protection of the animals, sea life, plants, land, water, and air.

- Because the population is small, the area has very little pollution.

- Some villagers make money by hunting wild animals in the rainforest and selling them to restaurants in other cities. Landwatch wants to preserve the wildlife. It wants locals to stop hunting the animals, but the locals need the extra money.

- The fishermen have taken too many fish from the ocean. Landwatch wants them to catch fewer fish and let the fish population grow again.

- Landwatch needs money to continue its rainforest research and to teach the locals how to preserve the environment.

Group C: Locals

Your group represents the needs of local residents.

- People in the village live a traditional way of life. The culture is based on their lives as fishermen, with many rituals, crafts, and customs. Some people are afraid these traditions will be lost if the village changes.

- The fishermen use the Coral Beach to bring in their fishing boats.

- There is a high unemployment rate in the village. There are fewer fish in the ocean now, so there is less work for the fishermen. There are not many other jobs for people in the village.

- The village is not well developed. It needs better roads and utilities (water, electricity, phones). The nearest hospital is a three-hour drive, and most villagers don't have cars. There is a small school, but it needs more teachers and supplies (textbooks, paper, pencils, etc.).

- Some villagers earn extra money by hunting wild animals in the rainforest and selling them to restaurants in the city. Landwatch is trying to stop people from doing this, but the locals need the extra money.

STEP 2: Form new groups of three, one student from Group A, one from Group B, and one from Group C. Each student explains the position of the group he or she is representing (for example, "I represent Royal Hotels, and we think . . ."). Work together to create a compromise proposal. Try to use the vocabulary, pronunciation, and language for making suggestions that you learned in the unit. Take notes in the chart.

COMPROMISE PROPOSAL		
THE HOTEL WILL / WON'T . . .	LANDWATCH WILL / WON'T . . .	THE VILLAGERS WILL / WON'T . . .
Example *will* ask Landwatch for permission to build a road	*will* consider the hotel's proposal **if** the hotel supports educational programs	*won't* hunt wild animals for money if they can get jobs in the hotel

STEP 3: Present the compromise proposals to the whole class.

Listen to the compromise proposals from the other groups. Be prepared to discuss these questions for each proposal:

1. Do you think the proposal presents a workable solution to the problem?

2. What additional ideas could be added to the proposal?

UNIT PROJECT

Some tourists use their vacation time to help others or help the environment. For example, a volunteer could go to a poor community and build homes for poor people. These types of vacations are called "service vacations" or "volunteer vacations."

STEP 1: Do research to find an example of a service vacation. You can . . .

- look for service vacations or volunteer vacations on the Internet.
- look for brochures or magazines about service vacations from environmental groups (for example, EarthWatch) or human aid groups (for example, Global Volunteers).

STEP 2: Prepare a short report to share with the class. Use the questions as a guide:

1. What is the destination of this vacation?

2. What can you do on this vacation?

3. Can people who choose this vacation really help the environment or the people who live nearby? If so, how? If not, why not?

4. Would you go on this vacation? Why or why not?

STEP 3: Present your report to the class.

ALTERNATIVE SPEAKING TOPICS

Discuss one of the topics. Use the vocabulary and grammar from the unit.

1. If you were a travel agent in your home country, what kinds of tours would you book? What areas would you take people to visit and why? What would the impact of tourism be on those areas?

2. For some places, tourism is the most important way to make money. For example, Thailand used to make most of its money from growing rice, but now more money comes from tourism. What are the pros and cons of relying on tourism as a source of money?

GO TO MyEnglishLab TO DISCUSS ONE OF THE ALTERNATIVE TOPICS, WATCH A VIDEO ABOUT ECOTOURISM, AND TAKE THE UNIT 6 ACHIEVEMENT TEST.

BEFORE YOU SAY "I Do"

1 FOCUS ON THE TOPIC

1. Look at the photo. What's happening?

2. What do you think this unit will be about?

3. Read the following statements about marriage. Do you agree or disagree with them? Discuss your opinions with a partner.

- In most marriages, only one person can get what he or she wants.
- To have a happy marriage, the couple must be good friends.
- You should choose your spouse[1] carefully before marriage, but after marriage you should accept his or her mistakes.

---

[1] **spouse:** husband or wife

GO TO MyEnglishLab TO CHECK WHAT YOU KNOW.

VOCABULARY

1 🎧 Read and listen to information about a prenuptial agreement. Notice the boldfaced words.

> A prenuptial agreement is a written agreement between two people who are going to tie the knot.[2] Most prenuptial agreements concern what will happen to a couple's money, property, or children if the marriage ends. It is used only if a problem **occurs** and the couple decides to get divorced. However, some prenuptial agreements also describe how the husband and wife must act during the marriage. Steve and Karen Parsons made this type of agreement. They wrote a **contract** with rules for how they must behave in almost every part of their daily lives.

MARRIAGE CONTRACT
Steve and Karen Parsons

1.0 Daily Habits
1.1 We will go to sleep by 11:00 P.M. and wake up by 6:00 A.M. on weekdays. Bedtime on weekends will be more **flexible**.
1.2 We will not drive over the speed limit and will always wear our seatbelts.
1.3 We will eat healthy food that is low in fat and sugar.

2.0 Household Chores
2.1 Meals: Karen will cook the meals. Steve will wash the dishes and clean the kitchen.
2.2 Cleaning: Steve will clean the house. Karen will take care of the garden.
2.3 Laundry: Dirty clothes must be put in the laundry bag. Steve will wash and dry the clothes. Karen will fold the clothes and put them away.
2.4 Shopping: Karen will do the grocery shopping. She will buy things on sale and not go over our weekly **budget**.

3.0 Communication
3.1 If something **bothers** us, we will talk about it immediately.
3.2 If we disagree about something, we will **work out** the problem and find a compromise.
3.3 We promise not to criticize each other's **quirks** or habits.

---

[1] **prenuptial:** before marriage (pronounced: /pre-'nep-shəl/)
[2] **tie the knot:** to get married

4.0 Children

4.1 We will wait for two years before we have a child. We will have two children.

4.2 After our first child is born, the partner who makes less money will quit his or her job and stay home with the child. The partner who makes more money will become the **breadwinner** for the family.

We each understand the other's **expectations** for how to behave in our marriage. We can **check up on** each other to make sure the other is following the rules.

Signed,

Steve Parsons　　　　　　　　　　　*Karen Parsons*

---

2 Match the words with the definitions. Write the correct letter.

_____ **1.** occur   **a.** to happen

_____ **2.** contract   **b.** to solve

_____ **3.** flexible   **c.** the person who earns money to support the family

_____ **4.** budget   **d.** to annoy

_____ **5.** bother   **e.** to find out what someone is doing

_____ **6.** work out   **f.** a legal agreement between two people

_____ **7.** quirk   **g.** a strange or unusual habit

_____ **8.** breadwinner   **h.** a belief or hope that something will happen

_____ **9.** expectation   **i.** a plan for how to spend money

_____ **10.** check up on   **j.** able to change easily in a new situation

GO TO MyEnglishLab FOR MORE VOCABULARY PRACTICE.

PREVIEW

Steve and Karen Parsons appear on a radio show to talk about their prenuptial agreement.

🎧 Listen to an excerpt from the interview. Read two questions the host will ask Steve and Karen later in the interview. How do you think they will answer? Write your predictions.

1. "So, I'd like to start off by asking you what everybody is probably wondering. Why did you decide to write this agreement?"

   Predicted answer: _____

2. "Do you think other couples should follow your example and write marriage contracts of their own?"

   Predicted answer: _____

MAIN IDEAS

1 🎧 Listen to the whole interview. Look again at your predictions from the Preview section. How did your predictions help you understand the interview?

2 In the interview, Steve and Karen discuss several problems that married people have. Check (✓) the four problems mentioned in the interview.

   ☐ 1. Different expectations about marriage

   ☐ 2. Problems with other family members

☐ **3.** Quirks that bother the other spouse

☐ **4.** Working too much

☐ **5.** Not knowing what the other spouse wants

☐ **6.** Disagreements about money

☐ **7.** Relationships with other men or women

DETAILS

🎧 Listen again. Read the statements. Write **T** (true) or **F** (false).

_____ **1.** Steve and Karen have a five-page prenuptial agreement.

_____ **2.** Both Steve and Karen have been married before.

_____ **3.** It bothered Steve when his ex-wife left her clothes lying on the floor.

_____ **4.** Karen thinks that working out a compromise is more romantic than flowers and candy.

_____ **5.** Karen says that the prenuptial agreement is like a business contract.

_____ **6.** Karen and Steve argue about their budget.

_____ **7.** Steve and Karen feel that they spend the same amount of time arguing as other couples do.

_____ **8.** Steve and Karen agree about all the rules in the prenuptial agreement.

_____ **9.** Steve and Karen feel that a prenuptial agreement could be useful for other couples.

GO TO MyEnglishLab *FOR MORE LISTENING PRACTICE.*

MAKE INFERENCES

INFERRING CERTAINTY FROM WORD CHOICE

A speaker may express feeling sure or less sure about an idea. The listener can infer the speaker's certainty by paying attention to word choice.

Certain

Our prenuptial agreement has **definitely** made us happier.

We **will never** fight.

Less Certain

Our prenuptial agreement has **most likely** made us happier.

I **doubt that** we will fight much.

🎧 Read and listen to the example. Notice the boldfaced word. Is the speaker certain or less certain?

Example

So, I'd like to start off by asking you what everybody is **probably** wondering: Why did you decide to write this agreement?

By using the word "probably" instead of a more definite word, the speaker shows that she is "less certain" about people's questions.

1 🎧 Listen to the excerpts. Fill in the blanks with the missing words. Is the speaker "certain" or "less certain" about his / her comments? Circle your answer.

Excerpt One

HOST: Well, I'm _____ that some people hearing this report will think

that this isn't very romantic.

The speaker is **certain / less certain** about the opinions of the audience.

Excerpt Two

STEVE: Yeah, it's unusual, but it _____ makes sense. We

_____ want someone home with our kids . . .

The speaker is **certain / less certain** about the plan for raising kids.

Excerpt Three

STEVE: Well, it's a lot of work to write something like this . . . but I think it

_____ be useful to a lot of people.

The speaker is **certain / less certain** about the usefulness of a contract for other couples.

2 Discuss your answers with a partner. Talk about the information that helped you find the answers.

EXPRESS OPINIONS

Work in a small group. Discuss the questions.

1. Do you agree or disagree with Steve and Karen's opinions about marriage? Work individually to make a list of the ideas that you agree and disagree with. Then discuss your ideas.

2. What would you say if your fiancé / fiancée[1] asked you to write a prenuptial agreement like Steve and Karen's? Why?

================================ GO TO MyEnglishLab TO GIVE YOUR OPINION ABOUT ANOTHER QUESTION.

LISTENING TWO REACTIONS TO THE PRENUPTIAL AGREEMENT

VOCABULARY

1 Read the advice and facts about marriage. Notice the boldfaced words.

1. If you have a problem, **open up** and discuss it calmly with your spouse.

2. Don't **blow up** and yell at your partner.

3. The decision to get married should be made carefully. Couples should not **rush into** it.

4. A marriage license is a **legal** document that shows that two people are married.

5. To get divorced, a couple must go to **court** and talk to the judge.

2 Match the boldfaced words with the definitions. Write the words.

_____ **a.** to say what you really think

_____ **b.** a place where decisions are made according to the law

_____ **c.** to become very angry

_____ **d.** to decide to do something too quickly

_____ **e.** allowed by the law

_____

[1] **fiancé / fiancée:** the man / woman you are going to marry

COMPREHENSION

🎧 Listen to different people calling the talk show to share their reactions to Steve and Karen's prenuptial agreement. Do they think the agreement is a good idea or a bad idea? Check (✓) each caller's opinion. Then identify the reason for the caller's opinion. Write the correct letter. One reason isn't mentioned in the listening.

Caller 1

Caller 2

Caller 3

Caller 4

Caller 5

	GOOD IDEA	BAD IDEA	REASON
CALLER 1	☐	☐	
CALLER 2	☐	☐	
CALLER 3	☐	☐	
CALLER 4	☐	☐	
CALLER 5	☐	☐	

Reasons

a. Couples learn to open up about their problems.

b. It helps couples think carefully before they marry.

c. Each spouse has to follow a budget.

d. It's not romantic.

e. It has too many details.

f. It's not legal.

GO TO MyEnglishLab FOR MORE VOCABULARY PRACTICE.

LISTENING SKILL

1 🎧 Listen to an excerpt from the lawyer's reaction to the marriage contract. What is the lawyer's opinion of the contract?

LISTENING FOR *BUT* TO SIGNAL DISAGREEMENT AND A CONTRASTING OPINION

To disagree politely, a speaker often acknowledges the other person's opinion and then introduces his or her own opinion with *but*.

For instance, if a speaker says *"That's a good point, but I disagree . . . ,"* the speaker's main point is "I disagree."

🎧 Read and listen to the example. Notice the word **but**, used to signal disagreement and introduce the speaker's main point. What is the speaker's main point?

Example

CALLER 5:   *Yeah, I know a lot of people might think that this contract idea is crazy, **but** I think . . . I think it could be useful to help couples decide if they really should get married.*

After the word *but*, the speaker says that the contract would be useful. This is the speaker's main point.

2 🎧 Listen to the excerpts. What is the speaker's main point? Circle the correct answer.

Excerpt One

The speaker's main point is that . . .

a. she's glad Karen and Steve are happy.

b. she doesn't want to sign a prenuptial agreement.

c. she doesn't think prenuptial agreements can make people happy.

Excerpt Two

The speaker's main point is that . . .

a. the contract is not necessary.

b. the contract has too many details.

c. the contract is a good idea.

(continued on next page)

Excerpt Three

The speaker's main point is that . . .

a. the contract is legal.

b. the contract looks like it is legal.

c. the contract is not legal.

--- GO TO MyEnglishLab FOR MORE SKILL PRACTICE.

CONNECT THE LISTENINGS

STEP 1: Organize

🎧 Listen to Listenings One and Two again. Then complete the chart with arguments for and against prenuptial agreements. Add an example to illustrate each argument.

LISTENING ONE: Arguments for Prenuptial Agreements	EXAMPLES
• help couples talk about problems	• *Karen—told Steve about problems with ex-husband*
• _____	• Caller 5—people rush into marriage without thinking
• make expectations clearer	• _____
• _____	• Karen and Steve—spend less time arguing

LISTENING TWO: Arguments Against Prenuptial Agreements	EXAMPLES
• too structured and not flexible	• *Karen and Steve—11:00 P.M. bedtime, can't go to bed earlier or later*
• _____	• Caller 1—if you love someone, you don't need to write things down
• too many details	• _____
• _____	• Caller 4—contract won't hold up in court

STEP 2: Synthesize

Work with a partner. Debate the topic of prenuptial agreements. One person takes the pro position (in favor) and the other person takes the con position (against). Use the reasons and examples from Step 1: Organize.

Switch partners and repeat the debate, with each person taking the opposite position.

--- GO TO MyEnglishLab TO CHECK WHAT YOU LEARNED.

VOCABULARY

REVIEW

1 Make words from the scrambled letters. Write one letter in each square. (Don't worry about the numbers below the boxes. You will use them in the next exercise.)

1. Problems often UCROC in a marriage when the husband and wife don't communicate well.

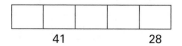

        41   28

2. When my wife and I have a problem, we ROKWTUO a solution we both agree on.

   33   12   30

3. We made a BUTDEG so we don't spend too much money.

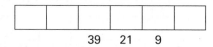

        39 21 9

4. It really STHEBOR me when my husband leaves dirty dishes in the sink.

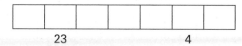

     23   4

5. I trust my wife, so I can really NOEPPU and tell her how I feel.

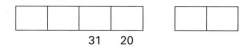

      31 20

6. Our marriage CATTOCNR states that if we have children, they will have the same last name as their mother.

        3   22

7. Traditionally, a husband is the DREWEBRANNI for the family.

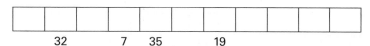

   32   7 35   19

8. My parents and I have different PAXTOETEINSC about whom I will marry.

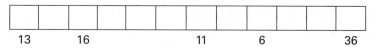

  13   16   11   6   36

(continued on next page)

9. I don't HCEKCPUNO my husband to see if he is following the contract. I trust him.

	26	24				42					

10. If a problem doesn't get solved, it gets bigger, and when this happens your wife might PLBOWU at you.

	2				15	

11. My lawyer said that a marriage contract is not a GLAEL document.

17		8	1	43

12. I took my prenuptial agreement to TCUOR, but the judge wouldn't read it.

			5	44

13. My parents told me, "Don't SHRUTOIN marriage. Take time to get to know each other."

34		38	14		40		25

14. It's easier to get along if both spouses are BELLIFEX and can compromise.

29		27		37			

15. Sometimes you don't learn about your spouse's KRQUIS until after marriage!

	18			10	

2 Figure out the saying about marriage. Copy the letters in the numbered squares from Exercise 1 to the squares below with the same numbers. Discuss with the class whether you agree with this saying.

		L		M												
1	2			3	4	5	6	7	8	9	10		11	12	13	

	A		Y			V			
14	15	16		17	18	19	20	21	

		G						A					A			
22	23		24	25	26	27	28	29	30	31	32	33	34	35	36	

				F	F	I			
37	38	39	40			41	42	43	44

1 Read the letter to an online advice columnist. Notice the boldfaced words.

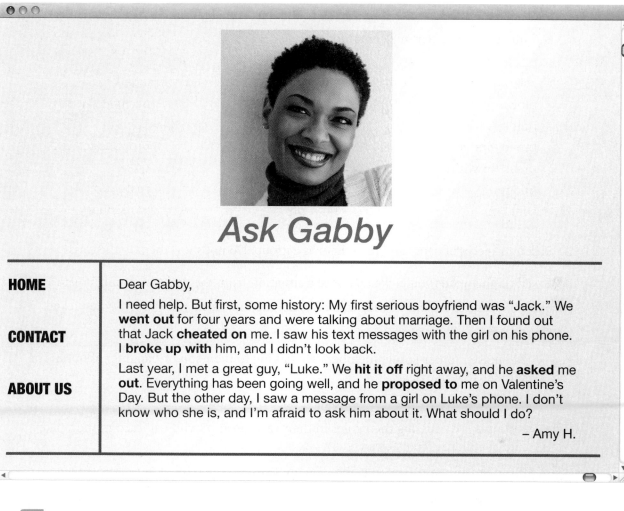

Ask Gabby

HOME **CONTACT** **ABOUT US**	Dear Gabby, I need help. But first, some history: My first serious boyfriend was "Jack." We **went out** for four years and were talking about marriage. Then I found out that Jack **cheated on** me. I saw his text messages with the girl on his phone. I **broke up with** him, and I didn't look back. Last year, I met a great guy, "Luke." We **hit it off** right away, and he **asked** me **out**. Everything has been going well, and he **proposed to** me on Valentine's Day. But the other day, I saw a message from a girl on Luke's phone. I don't know who she is, and I'm afraid to ask him about it. What should I do? <div align="right">– Amy H.</div>

2 Work with a partner. Write the correct letters to complete the summary of Amy's relationship history. Discuss Amy's problem with your partner. What should she do? Why?

____ 1. Amy ____ with "Jack."

____ 2. He ____.

____ 3. Amy found out and ____.

____ 4. Then Amy met "Luke," and they ____.

____ 5. Luke ____.

____ 6. Then he ____.

a. liked each other right away

b. asked Amy to marry him

c. had a secret relationship with someone else

d. ended their relationship

e. was in a relationship

f. invited Amy to go on a date

CREATE

Work in a small group. Create a role play. Follow the steps.

1. Write each word or phrase from the word box on a small piece of paper. Fold the papers and mix them together in a container.

ask out	check up on	legal
blow up	contract	occur
bother	court	open up
breadwinner	expectation	propose to
break up with	flexible	quirk
budget	go out	rush into
cheat on	hit it off	work out

2. Pick four pieces of paper and read them as a group. Do not show them to the class.

3. Based on the words you picked, choose a situation from the list. As a group, create a role play about the situation. In your role play, use the four vocabulary words you picked.

Situations

- Parents and other family members are talking to their son or daughter about his or her plans for marriage.
- Friends are discussing what kind of spouse they want.
- A couple is discussing their roles in their relationship (who will earn money, take care of children, cook, clean, etc.).
- Family members are talking about a couple that is breaking up or getting a divorce.
- Make up a situation.

4. Practice the role play and then perform it for the class.

As you watch the role plays by the other groups, listen carefully for the four vocabulary words they use. Write them down. When the role play is finished, check to see whether your words match the pieces of paper that the performers picked.

GO TO MyEnglishLab FOR MORE VOCABULARY PRACTICE.

GRAMMAR

1 Read the conversation. Notice the boldfaced **comparatives and equatives** and answer the questions.

> **KAISA:** How's married life?
>
> **NORIKO:** It's **as wonderful as** living together, but different.
>
> **KAISA:** How so?
>
> **NORIKO:** Well, I think our relationship is **stronger**. We're **less worried** about breaking up, and we're **more careful** about saving money.
>
> **KAISA:** Sounds like married life is **better than** being single.
>
> **NORIKO:** It is.

1. Which phrase expresses the idea that two things are *equal*?

2. Which phrase(s) express the idea of *more*? Which expresses the idea of *less*?

COMPARATIVES AND EQUATIVES	
1. Use **equatives** to express the idea of *equal*.	Our relationship is **as strong as** it was 10 years ago.
2. Use **comparative adjectives** to express the idea of *more*.	Our relationship is **stronger than** it was 10 years ago. My second marriage is **happier than** my first. As a gift, flowers are **more romantic than** books.
3. Use **comparative adjectives** to express the idea of *less*.	My wife is **less patient than** I am. Our marriage is **not as strong as** it used to be.
4. There are some irregular **comparative** forms.	**Adjective** **Comparative** *bad* *worse* *good* *better*
5. It's not necessary to mention both parts of the comparison when the meaning is clear.	Our relationship is **stronger**. Flowers are **more romantic**.

2 Complete the conversation. Use comparatives and equatives. The + sign means more. The − sign means less. The = sign means equal.

KAISA: I'm (1) ___*less interested*___ (interested −) than you in settling down. I like my freedom too much.

NORIKO: I guess my life is (2) _____ (free −). It's

(3) _____ (easy +) for Greg to plan if he knows what I'm doing.

So I call from the office if my workday is (4) _____ (late +)

than usual.

KAISA: See. That's what I mean. I'm (5) _____ (happy +) when I can

come and go as I please.

NORIKO: But for me, being single is way (6) _____ (stressful +) than

being married. It's a lot (7) _____ (difficult +) to make decisions

about important stuff if you don't have someone to talk to. Married life is lot

(8) _____ (good +).

KAISA: Well, I'm glad it's working for you. Maybe one day I'll find the right guy, get

married, and be (9) _____ (happy =) you.

NORIKO: Maybe.

3 Work in a small group. Discuss the questions "Is it better to be married or single? Why?" Use the adjectives from the box and add your own.

Example

STUDENT A: I think it's *more difficult* to be single than to be married. If you're single, you're always looking for someone.

STUDENT B: That's true. I think married people aren't *as lonely as* single people.

STUDENT C: I know what you're saying, but . . .

bad	difficult	happy	serious
busy	easy	lonely	stressful
comfortable	free	responsible	strong
concerned	good	romantic	worried

GO TO MyEnglishLab FOR MORE GRAMMAR PRACTICE.

PRONUNCIATION

CONTRASTIVE STRESS

When we want to emphasize a difference, we stress the words that show the difference. This kind of emphasis is called *contrastive stress*. We also use contrastive stress to show that some information is correct and other information is incorrect.

🎧 Read and listen to the examples. Note how the boldfaced words are emphasized.

Examples

*I do the **laundry**, and **Steve** does the **dishes**.*

*I want to hear **good** news, **not bad** news.*

a)	Emphasize words that show a contrast (a difference).	🎧 *My **wife drives** to work, and **I** take the **bus**.*
b)	Emphasize words that show correct and incorrect information.	🎧 *Your appointment is **tomorrow, not today**.*
c)	To emphasize a word, say the word: • on a high pitch (tone) • louder • longer	🎧 *Tell me the **good** news [not the bad news].* 🎧 *Tell me the **GOOD** news.* 🎧 *Tell me the **g o o o d** news.*

1 🎧 Listen to each sentence. Underline the word that is emphasized. Then circle **a** or **b** to choose the meaning of the sentence.

1. <u>Karen</u> will do the grocery shopping.

    a. not Steve   **b.** not the laundry

2. Karen will always use a shopping list.

    a. not Steve   **b.** not sometimes

3. Nothing will be left on the floor in the bedroom.

    a. not on the table   **b.** not in the living room

4. On weekdays, we will go to bed at 11:00 p.m.

    a. not on weekends   **b.** not 9:00 p.m.

5. We will wait three years before buying a house.

    a. not two years   **b.** not a car

6. Karen will make a list of groceries every week.

    a. not Steve   **b.** not whenever she remembers

7. We will spend at least 15 minutes a day talking with each other.

    a. not less than 15 minutes   **b.** not with our relatives

8. Steve will figure out directions before we start a trip.

    a. not Karen   **b.** not after we start

9. We will eat healthy food that's low in fat and sugar.

    a. not junk food   **b.** both fat and sugar

10. We will update this agreement every year.

    a. not our lawyers   **b.** not every two years

2 Work with a partner. Student A says the sentences from Exercise 1, using word stress to show either meaning **a** or meaning **b**. Student B listens and guesses the meaning of the sentences. Then switch roles and repeat.

Example

STUDENT A: Number one. Karen will do the **grocery** shopping.

STUDENT B: That means "not the laundry," right?

STUDENT A: Yes.

3 Work with your partner. Each sentence has two sets of words that are contrasted with each other. Read the sentences and circle the first set of words that are contrasted. Then underline the second set. Take turns reading the sentences aloud, using contrastive stress.

1. (Steve's) been married <u>twice</u>, and (Karen's) been married <u>once</u>.

2. Many of the rules deal with money; only a few deal with other situations.

3. Steve takes care of the car, and Karen does the housework.

4. Getting married is easy, but living together afterward is more difficult.

5. On weekends, Karen gets up early, and Steve gets up late.

6. When it comes to food, Steve likes Japanese, and Karen likes Mexican.

7. One couple got marriage counseling, but the other couple got a divorce.

8. Most couples make verbal agreements; only a few want written agreements.

SPEAKING SKILL

TRANSITIONS IN ORAL PRESENTATIONS

We use *transitions* to make oral presentations clear. Transitions can be used to introduce main ideas (A) and supporting points (B).

A. Transitions for Introducing Main Ideas

1 🎧 Read and listen to the introductions to oral presentations. Underline the main idea that will be discussed in each presentation. Then circle the transitions used to introduce the main idea. Compare your answers with the class.

1. Some people think that prenuptial agreements are a crazy idea, but in my opinion they can help couples think about the realities of marriage. Today, I'd like to talk about the advantages of prenuptial agreements.

2. There's a new trend in love and marriage: prenuptial agreements. You may have heard of them, but do you really know what they are? I'm going to define prenuptial agreements and explain why they're becoming popular.

3. Prenuptial agreements may seem like a good idea for Hollywood movie stars. They go through two or three marriages in a lifetime. But for regular people like you and me, these contracts are a mistake. The question that I'll discuss today is: "What's the problem with prenuptial agreements?"

B. Transitions for Introducing Supporting Points

2 Read transitions for introducing supporting points. Complete the outlines on the next page with transitions for introducing the main idea. Then decide whether the supporting points are equally important or not and add those transitions. Read your answers to a partner.

POINTS OF EQUAL IMPORTANCE	POINTS FROM MOST TO LEAST IMPORTANT
One reason is . . .	The most important reason is . . .
Another reason is . . .	Another important reason is . . .
And last but not least[1] . . .	A final reason is . . .

---

[1] **last but not least:** the last point is not less important than the others

A. Main idea: _____ the benefits of a prenuptial agreement.

Supporting point 1: _____ it encourages couples to think carefully before they get married.

Supporting point 2: _____ it helps couples talk about things that are important to them.

Supporting point 3: _____ it makes expectations clearer.

B. Main idea: _____: "What is wrong with a prenuptial agreement?"

Supporting point 1: _____ it shows that couples don't trust each other.

Supporting point 2: _____ it doesn't allow people to change and grow.

Supporting point 3: _____ it makes couples think about divorce before they even get married.

▪▪▪▪▪▪▪▪▪▪▪▪▪▪▪▪ *GO TO* MyEnglishLab *FOR MORE SKILL PRACTICE AND TO CHECK WHAT YOU LEARNED.*

FINAL SPEAKING TASK

In an oral presentation a speaker prepares a speech and presents it to an audience.

In this activity, you will give a 3–5-minute oral presentation on a controversial topic related to marriage.

Follow the steps. Try to use the vocabulary, grammar, pronunciation, and listening and speaking skills that you learned in the unit.*

STEP 1: Choose a topic for your presentation. You may choose one of the following topics or think of your own topic.

- living together before marriage

- the rights of unmarried couples

- using dating services to find a spouse (Internet sites, speed dating)

- arranged marriages vs. love marriages

- mixed marriages (religion, age, language, culture, race)

- types of families (blended,[1] single parent)

- living situations in marriage (long-distance marriages, living with relatives)

- divorce

- gay marriage

- Other: _____

Write a sentence stating your opinion about the topic: _____

_____

Example

Topic: *Prenuptial Agreements*

Opinion: *I think prenuptial agreements are a good way to prepare for marriage.*

---

*For Alternative Speaking Tasks, see page 179.

[1] **blended family:** a family formed when two families are joined by marriage; a stepfamily

STEP 2: Plan your presentation using the outline. Practice giving your presentation to a friend or in front of a mirror. Or videotape yourself with a cell phone or computer and review the video.

Introduction (1/2–1 minute)
- Introduce the topic
- Give background information
- State your opinion

Body (2–3 minutes)

Give two or three reasons for your opinion
- State each reason
- Explain each reason using details and examples

Conclusion (1/2 minute)
- Restate your opinion
- Make a concluding statement (e.g., summary of reasons, prediction for the future, quotation, question)

STEP 3: Give your presentation to the class. When presenting, look at the audience and use your outline as a guide. Speak loudly and clearly.

Listening Task

Listen to your classmates' presentations. During each presentation, write down one question that you could ask the presenter at the end of his / her speech.

UNIT PROJECT

STEP 1: In this activity you will research an alternative marriage practice. Choose a topic from the box or think of your own.

civil unions	Internet brides	polygamy
dowry	matchmakers	serial monogamy
gay marriage		

STEP 2: Do online research to find a documentary about the topic you chose. Then watch the documentary and prepare a presentation to explain the marriage practice to the class. As part of your presentation, create a visual (for example, a chart with statistics or a poster with pictures) to show to the class.

Here are some questions to guide your presentation:

1. What is _____?

2. What interesting information did you learn from the video? (Give specific facts and statistics.)

3. What controversial issues arise from this marriage practice?

4. After watching the video, what is your opinion about _____?

STEP 3: Meet in small groups with students who chose a different marriage practice. Talk about your topic and show your visual. Then answer questions from the group.

ALTERNATIVE SPEAKING TOPICS

Look at the graph and discuss the topics. Use the vocabulary and grammar from the unit.

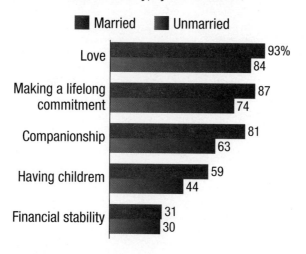

Why Get Married?
Percent saying each is a very important
reason to marry, by marital status

■ Married   ■ Unmarried

Reason	Married	Unmarried
Love	93%	84
Making a lifelong commitment	87	74
Companionship	81	63
Having childrem	59	44
Financial stability	31	30

Asked of married and unmarried separately, n = 1,306 for
married and 1,385 for unmarried.
Source: Pew Research Center (2010)

1. According to the survey, what do Americans feel is the most important reason to get married? What is the least important?

2. How do you think people in your home country would answer question 1? Is there a difference? Why or why not?

3. In your opinion, what two things listed on the chart are the most important reasons for getting married? What are the two least important reasons? Explain your opinion.

GO TO MyEnglishLab TO DISCUSS ONE OF THE ALTERNATIVE TOPICS, WATCH A VIDEO ABOUT MARRIAGE, AND TAKE THE UNIT 7 ACHIEVEMENT TEST.

REDUCING YOUR CARBON
Footprint

1 FOCUS ON THE TOPIC

1. Look at the photo. Is this something happening now, in the near future, or in the distant future?

2. Over the past 100 years, temperatures and weather patterns around the world have changed. There are more storms, floods, and extreme temperatures. What extreme weather have you heard about or experienced?

3. Scientists believe that climate change is caused by global warming. Global warming is an increase in temperatures all over the world. What do you think might be some of the causes of global warming?

GO TO MyEnglishLab TO CHECK WHAT YOU KNOW.

LISTENING ONE | LIVING SMALL

VOCABULARY

1 🎧 Read and listen to the article about how our lifestyle can affect global warming. Notice the boldfaced words.

PERSONAL CARBON FOOTPRINT

Your *personal carbon footprint* is the amount of carbon dioxide (CO_2)[1] that you put into the air when you drive a car, fly in an airplane, or use electricity made by burning coal[2] or gas.

CO_2 and other **greenhouse gases** have a serious impact on the environment. They make Earth warmer, causing climate change.

Even the food you eat affects your personal carbon footprint. A diet that includes a lot of meat creates a bigger footprint, while the footprint of a vegetarian diet is smaller. This is because a lot of **resources** are used to raise animals and **transport** meat from the farm to your table.

Ways to Reduce Your Personal Carbon Footprint

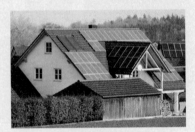

Install **solar panels** to make electricity for your house.

Grow vegetables in a raised **bed** in your garden.

Foods: sources of greenhouse gas emissions

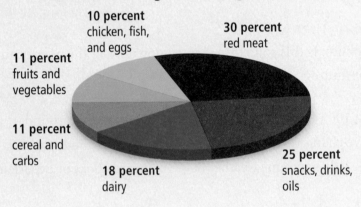

10 percent
chicken, fish, and eggs

30 percent
red meat

11 percent
fruits and vegetables

11 percent
cereal and carbs

18 percent
dairy

25 percent
snacks, drinks, oils

---

[1] **carbon dioxide:** often called *CO_2* in speech and writing
[2] **coal:** a hard, black mineral that is dug out of the ground and burned to produce heat

What can we do to protect the environment for future **generations**? **Collectively**, we must reduce our energy **consumption**. Start with simple changes to reduce your own carbon footprint. For example, skip a serving of meat each week. It may seem like **a drop in the bucket**, but it's equal to driving 320 miles (515 kilometers) in a car.

Protect and plant trees. **Dense** forests around the world are being cut down to make room for farms. This causes a faster increase in greenhouse gasses. Trees have a positive impact on climate by taking CO_2 out of the air. Forests take in nearly 40 percent of human-made CO_2.

2 Complete the definition. Circle the best answer.

1. **greenhouse gas:** a gas, especially carbon dioxide (CO_2) or methane (CH_4), that traps _____ above the Earth and causes global warming

   a. water

   b. heat

   c. pollution

2. **resource:** a supply of something _____ such as land, oil, or coal

   a. useful

   b. expensive

   c. big

3. **transport:** to _____ goods or people _____

   a. keep . . . in one place

   b. take . . . from one place to another in a vehicle

   c. look for . . . that can be helpful

4. **generation:** all people _____

   a. living together

   b. of about the same age

   c. in the same country

(continued on next page)

5. **collectively:** _____

   a. as a group

   b. alone

   c. with friends

6. **consumption:** the _____ of energy, oil, or electricity

   a. use

   b. cost

   c. selling

7. **a drop in the bucket:** an action that has _____ effect

   a. a big

   b. little or no

   c. an unexpected

8. **solar panel:** equipment that makes energy from the _____

   a. sun

   b. wind

   c. ocean

9. **(raised) bed:** an area in a garden that is used to _____

   a. keep chickens

   b. collect trash

   c. grow plants

10. **dense:** made of a lot of things that are very _____

    a. small

    b. far apart

    c. close together

GO TO MyEnglishLab FOR MORE VOCABULARY PRACTICE.

PREVIEW

Julia Peters is trying to leave a small carbon footprint. She describes her life in a podcast.

🎧 Listen to an excerpt from Julia's podcast. Which topics will she mention in the podcast? Check (✓) your predictions.

_____ **a.** driving an hour to work

_____ **b.** growing food

_____ **c.** using solar energy

_____ **d.** cutting forests to build houses

_____ **e.** living with other people

_____ **f.** starting a large chicken factory

MAIN IDEAS

1 🎧 Listen to the whole podcast. Look again at your predictions from the Preview section. How did your predictions help you to understand the podcast?

2 Complete each statement. Circle the correct answer.

1. Julia lives with a small carbon footprint to _____.

   a. save money

   b. protect Earth for future generations

   c. live a healthy life

2. Julia grows her own food because _____.

   a. food from the store has been transported from far away

   b. the stores near her house don't have fresh vegetables

   c. her garden has many raised beds

3. Julia has solar panels to _____.

   a. produce all the energy for her house

   b. avoid using energy that comes from coal

   c. encourage her neighbors to use clean energy

4. Julia shares her house with other people because _____.

   a. she likes living with friends

   b. the government gives her money for sharing

   c. it saves energy

5. Julia believes that the efforts of _____ can help to make a change.

   a. the government

   b. one person

   c. her family

DETALS

🎧 Listen again. All the statements contain some FALSE information. Cross out the parts that are untrue and write corrections.

1. The speaker's name is Julia ~~Smith~~. *Peters*

2. Julia lives in San Francisco, California.

3. She lives in an old house.

4. Julia says that she grows carrots, basil, and squash in her yard.

5. For the average American, the food he / she eats has traveled 500 miles.

6. In the summer Julia's chickens lay about two eggs a day.

7. If we don't reduce our coal consumption, the average temperature of the earth will increase two or three degrees.

8. There are three people living in Julia's house.

9. It's difficult for one person to have an impact on climate change when there are 4 billion people on the planet.

GO TO MyEnglishLab FOR MORE LISTENING PRACTICE.

MAKE INFERENCES

INFERRING CONTRAST FROM CONTEXT

A speaker may indirectly express a contrast between two situations. The listener can infer the contrasting ideas based on the context.

🎧 In the listening, Julia implies that her life is different from the lives of most Americans. Notice the boldfaced words.

Example

Here in the backyard, you can see, *it's not much of a yard. There's not much grass.* We've taken out most of the grass to put in raised beds so that we can grow more of our own food.

Julia is *implying* that her yard is different from most other yards and that most Americans have grass instead of raised beds.

1 🎧 Listen to the excerpts. Julia explains what she does and implies what most Americans do. Complete the chart.

	WHAT JULIA DOES	WHAT MOST AMERICANS DO
EXCERPT 1		
EXCERPT 2		

2 Work with a partner. Talk about the information that helped you find the answers.

EXPRESS OPINIONS

Discuss the questions with the class.

1. What do you think about Julia's way of "living small"? Would you want to live like she does? Why or why not?

2. Are Julia's efforts just "a drop in the bucket," or do you think that her actions can have an impact on global warming?

3. In what ways is Julia's lifestyle different from the way people live in your home country? In what ways is it similar?

━━━━━━━━━━━━━━━━━━━━━━━━━━━━ GO TO MyEnglishLab TO GIVE YOUR OPINION ABOUT ANOTHER QUESTION.

VOCABULARY

1 Read the fact sheet. Notice the boldfaced words.

FACT SHEET

1. The motor vehicle **industry** is one of the top 10 areas of manufacturing in the United States.

2. **Factories** in China produce 25 percent of the automobiles in the world.

3. Newer cars are more **energy-efficient**, so they need less gasoline than older cars.

4. New **technology**, such as radar to help cars drive backwards, will make cars easier and safer to drive.

5. Newer cars use less gasoline, and this reduces their carbon dioxide (CO_2) **emissions**.

2 Match the boldfaced words with the definitions. Write the words.

_____ **a.** gases that go into the air

_____ **b.** using less of a resource (gas, oil, water)

_____ **c.** buildings where products are made by machines

_____ **d.** a group of businesses that make the same type of product

_____ **e.** machines that are based on modern knowledge of science and computers

COMPREHENSION

🎧 Listen to the speech at an environment rally. Then answer the questions.

1. Label the percentages in the graph with the source of CO_2 emissions.

   a. making electricity

   b. transportation

   c. industry (businesses and factories)

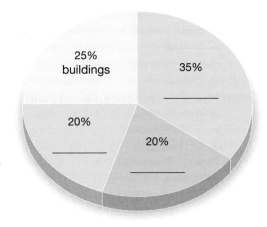

2. What is the main point the speaker is trying to make? Circle the correct answer.

   a. Factories and businesses produce a lot of pollution.

   b. Government and industry need to do more to reduce carbon emissions.

   c. Individuals should do more to reduce their personal carbon footprints.

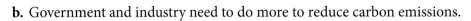

GO TO MyEnglishLab FOR MORE VOCABULARY PRACTICE.

LISTENING SKILL

1 🎧 Listen to an excerpt of the speech "A Call to Action." What words or phrases does the speaker repeat?

REPETITION TO EMPHASIZE A POINT

Speakers repeat words, phrases, and grammatical patterns to make their points stronger or to signal that they are important. The repetition also creates a rhythm (like a song or poem) that sounds good to the listener. Repetition is especially common in public speeches.

🎧 Listen to the example. Notice the boldfaced words and the underlined patterns.

Example

It's not enough for individuals to **change**. <u>We need</u> governments <u>to</u> **change**. <u>We need</u> industry <u>to</u> **change**. <u>We need</u> big **changes** if we want to stop global warming from destroying our planet.

The speaker repeats the word *change* and the pattern *we need _____ to _____*. The repetition makes the statement stronger and emphasizes the need for change.

2 🎧 Listen to the excerpts. Fill in the missing words in the repeated grammatical patterns. Then answer the questions.

Excerpt One

_____ government and industry _____ together to lower these emissions. _____ new, cleaner technology to heat our homes, power our factories, and _____ the lights on.

1. What words and / or grammatical patterns are repeated? _____

2. What ideas is the speaker trying to emphasize? _____

Excerpt Two

_____ government and industry _____ together to build more energy-efficient cars and trucks. _____ more public transportation.

1. What words and / or grammatical patterns are repeated? _____

2. What ideas is the speaker trying to emphasize? _____

GO TO MyEnglishLab FOR MORE SKILL PRACTICE.

STEP 1: Organize

Listen to Listenings One and Two again. Then complete the chart with ways to reduce carbon dioxide emissions.

	LISTENING ONE: Living Small	LISTENING TWO: A Call to Action
INDIVIDUALS	• Grow _____ • Use _____ • Live _____	• Reduce _____ • Tell _____
GOVERNMENT AND INDUSTRY		• Work _____ • Develop _____ • Build _____ • Reduce _____

STEP 2: Synthesize

Form two groups, Group A and Group B, to have a jigsaw discussion. Follow the steps.

1. Work with a partner in your group. Discuss the question assigned to your group. Use the information from Step 1: Organize.

   Group A: What can individuals do to reduce carbon dioxide emissions?

   Group B: What can government and industry do to reduce carbon dioxide emissions?

2. Find a partner in the other group. Work in pairs with one person from Group A and one person from Group B.

3. Take turns explaining the answer to your group's question to your partner. Use information from Step 1: Organize.

4. Change partners two more times so that you talk to three people total.

GO TO MyEnglishLab TO CHECK WHAT YOU LEARNED.

VOCABULARY

REVIEW

Complete the statements. Use the words from the box.

emissions	resources	transported

1. _____ from burning coal increase greenhouse gases.

2. We increase our personal carbon footprint when we eat food that is _____ long distances to get to our grocery stores.

3. The sun and the wind are two natural _____ that produce clean energy.

consumption	dense	raised beds	solar panels

4. I live in a group house with five other people, so you might say that I enjoy _____ living.

5. In our backyard, we grow food in _____.

6. Our electricity bill decreased when we put _____ on our roof.

7. I try to reduce my _____ of gasoline by riding my bike instead of driving my car.

energy-efficient	factories	industry	technology

8. Newer, more _____ cars use less fuel than old cars.

9. Cars make CO_2 emissions, and the _____ that make cars also produce emissions.

10. The automobile _____ has made changes to reduce CO_2 emissions, but it needs to do more.

11. Modern factories can become more efficient by using computers and other new _____.

(continued on next page)

| a drop in the bucket | collectively | generations | greenhouse gases |

12. We are beginning to see some of the effects of _____, but we won't know the full impact of climate change on the environment for many years.

13. If we don't stop global warming, future _____ will have to deal with the effects of climate change.

14. When I think of the big problem of global warming, the little things I do to reduce my footprint often seem like _____.

15. If individuals, government, and industry work _____, it is possible that the effects of global warming can be reversed.

EXPAND

1 Complete the chart with the missing word forms. Use a dictionary to help you.

NOUN	VERB	ADJECTIVE
transportation	transport	—
consumption		—
emissions		—
	—	energy-efficient
generation		—
	—	dense
resource	—	
industry	—	
technology	—	

2 Read the sentence pairs. Each sentence has a different form of the same word (for example, **transportation, transport**). Complete each sentence. Write the correct word form. Be sure to use the correct form of each word (singular or plural noun, subject-verb agreement).

1. I use buses, trains, and other kinds of public __*transportation*__ to get to and from work.

   I use my car when I have to __*transport*__ large or heavy things.

2. The sun is an important _____ for people who use solar energy.

   My brother is very _____. He found a government program to pay for his solar panels.

3. Trees can help to prevent global warming because they _____ CO_2.

   To protect our forests, we should reduce our _____ of paper.

4. _____ needs to do more to stop global warming.

   The air is polluted because we live in an _____ area.

5. Traveling by public transportation is more _____ than traveling in a personal car.

   The _____ of automobiles has increased in recent years with new electric and hybrid gas / electric cars.

6. New _____ for solar and wind energy will reduce the cost of those energy sources.

   There have been many _____ changes in the automobile industry over the past 100 years.

7. Climate change is caused by carbon _____ from burning coal, oil, and natural gas.

   Wood stoves also _____ carbon dioxide.

8. Cities are _____ living areas. People live close together in small spaces.

   The _____ of cities encourages people to use public transportation. Parking can be difficult, so people often find it more convenient to take buses and trains.

9. Future _____ will have to deal with the effects of climate change.

   Luckily scientists are discovering new ways to _____ power from the wind and the sea.

Work in a small group. Each student reads one of the statements aloud. The other students agree or disagree and explain why.

Agreeing / Disagreeing Language

I agree / disagree with this statement because . . .

I think / don't think _____ because . . .

I think this is / isn't a good idea because . . .

Use the vocabulary from the box in your answers. Check off the words as you use them.

collectively	energy-efficient factory	resourceful
consume	generate	solar panels
density	greenhouse gases	technology
a drop in the bucket	industry	transportation
emissions	raised beds	

Statements

1. New technology will solve the problem of climate change.

2. Industries should pay extra for the energy that they consume and the emissions that they release.

3. To reduce greenhouse gases, more countries should generate their energy from nuclear power.

4. All countries should limit the number of cars on the road and increase public transportation.

5. Even if individuals work collectively to reduce their personal carbon footprints, their efforts are still just a drop in the bucket.

GO TO MyEnglishLab FOR MORE VOCABULARY PRACTICE.

GRAMMAR

1 Read the interview. Notice the boldfaced **modals of necessity**. Then answer the questions.

HOST: What do individuals **have to** do to reduce their personal carbon footprint?

ENVIRONMENTAL ACTIVIST (EA): Well, we all **have to** drive less. We also need better public transportation so that we **don't have to** take our cars everywhere.

HOST: What else?

EA: Everyone **must** work together. We can't solve this problem alone. And we **must not** wait too long to make these changes—or else our climate will change forever.

1. What is the difference between *have to* and *must*? _____

   _____

2. What is the difference between *doesn't have to* and *must not*? _____

   _____

MODALS OF NECESSITY	
1. Use *have to* and *must* to tell when something is necessary. *Have to* is usually used in conversation and informal writing. *Must* is used most often in writing. NOTE: *Must* is stronger than *have to*.	We **have to** find ways to reduce emissions. We **must** stop global warming.
2. Use the correct form of *have to* for all tenses. Use *must* only for present and future tenses.	We **have to** make changes today. We **had to** start making changes years ago. We'll **have to** make more changes in the future. We **must** make changes today. We **must** make more changes in the future.

(continued on next page)

3. Use *have to* for questions. NOTE: *Must* is almost never used in questions.	What *do* individuals *have to* do? *Do* they *have to* stop driving?
4. Use *don't / doesn't have to* when something is not necessary (when there is a choice). Use *must not* when something is prohibited (when there is no choice). NOTE: In spoken English, *can't* is often used instead of *must not*.	We *don't have to* drive everywhere. We *must not / can't* wait too long to make changes.

2 Read the rest of the interview. Circle the correct answers.

HOST: What do businesses have to do to reduce emissions?

EA: First of all, business leaders **(1) must / don't have to** find new ways to reduce emissions from industry.

HOST: Will that cost a lot?

EA: Reducing emissions **(2) can't / doesn't have to** be expensive. In fact, businesses often save money.

HOST: How can our government help?

EA: Governments **(3) don't have to / must not** ignore the emissions problem. They **(4) can't / have to** create new laws to help reduce emissions.

HOST: Do we need new taxes to pay for this?

EA: No, we **(5) don't have to / must** have new taxes. There are other ways to raise money.

HOST: Any other thoughts?

EA: Sometimes people feel that this problem is impossible to solve, but we **(6) must not / don't have to** quit. And we **(7) must / can't** have everyone's help.

HOST: We're out of time, so we **(8) don't have to / have to** stop now. Thanks very much.

EA: Thank you.

3 Work with a partner. Read the list of suggestions and discuss how to reduce our personal carbon footprints. Use **have to / must**, **don't have to**, and **must not / can't**.

Example

STUDENT A: I think that we *must* build more public transportation.

STUDENT B: Yeah, I agree. We *have to* stop driving everywhere. We *can't* rely on cars so much.

Suggestions

1. build more public transportation

2. stop using electricity

3. ignore the problem of global warming

4. buy solar panels

5. stop using gasoline-powered cars

6. reduce factory emissions

7. drive big cars

8. ride bicycles

GO TO MyEnglishLab *FOR MORE GRAMMAR PRACTICE.*

PRONUNCIATION

INTONATION—ARE YOU FINISHED?

When you finish speaking, your voice should fall to a low note. When you have more to say but need some time to think, your voice doesn't fall to a low note—it stays on the same note as the previous word.

🎧 Listen to the way *I know* is pronounced in this conversation.

Example

A: If you're worried about the environment, you shouldn't drive to work.

B: I know.

A: You should take the bus.

B: I know . . . but I think it's faster when I drive.

You can use *I know* to agree or disagree. When we use *I know* to disagree, we often follow it with *but*.

1 🎧 Listen to the sentences. Is the speaker finished or not? If the speaker is finished, put a period (.) after the sentence. If the speaker is going to continue, put an ellipsis (. . .). Check your answers with a partner's.

1. I'm going to start riding my bike to work

2. I'm not going to use the air conditioner so much

3. I'm going to volunteer to clean up the park

4. I always turn off the lights

5. I drive to school once a week

6. I'm going to buy a hybrid[1]

7. I'm going to vote for green candidates

8. I'm going to recycle bottles and cans

---

[1] **hybrid:** A car that uses electric power at lower speeds and gasoline power at higher speeds. It produces less pollution.

2 Look at the unfinished sentences in Exercise 1. Choose a sentence and finish it. Say your sentence to the class.

3 Work with a partner. Practice using your voice to let your partner know whether you've finished speaking or not. Read the sentences in Exercise 1 to your partner. Let your voice fall if your sentence is finished. Don't let your voice fall if your sentence isn't finished. Your partner will tell you whether he or she thinks your sentence is finished or not. Then switch roles.

4 Read statements about the environment to your partner. Your partner gives his or her opinion, agreeing with **I know** or disagreeing with **I know, but** . . .

Student A's Statements

1. I don't think there's anything we can do about CO_2 levels. We all produce carbon dioxide when we breathe.

2. Wealthy countries create more pollution than poorer countries. They should have to pay to clean it up.

3. I'm worried about global warming, but I don't know if I can do anything to make a difference.

Student B's Statements

1. A lot of people in the automobile industry are going to lose their jobs if we raise taxes on gasoline.

2. A lot of storms hit coastal areas. The government shouldn't permit new building in coastal areas.

3. I need a new car, and I'd like to buy a hybrid. But they're more expensive than gas-powered cars.

SPEAKING SKILL

STRATEGIES FOR INTERRUPTING POLITELY

During a discussion you can politely interrupt the speaker and take a turn. A person might interrupt to share an idea or opinion, to ask a question, or to ask the speaker to repeat.

Sounds and Gestures	Words to Ask for Clarification / Explanation		Words to Make a Comment
Clear your throat (say "ahem").	*I'm sorry, could you . . . ?*	*. . . repeat that*	*I'd like to . . .*
Raise your hand.	*Could you . . . please?*	*. . . explain that*	*. . . add something.*
Raise your index finger.	*Excuse me, could you . . . ?*	*. . . say that again*	*. . . make a point.*
	Excuse me, can I . . . ?	*. . . ask a question*	*But . . .*
Make eye contact with the speaker.	*I'm sorry, can I . . . ?*	*. . . ask something*	*Can I say something?*

Strategies for Holding the Floor

If you are speaking and someone interrupts, you can "hold the floor," or keep talking, if you aren't ready to be interrupted.

Sounds and Gestures	Words for Holding the Floor
Keep talking.	*Just a minute / second.*
Speak louder.	*Hold on a minute / second.*
Don't look at the person interrupting.	*Let me finish, please.*
Put your hand up to show that you want the other person to wait.	*I'm not done yet.*

NOTE: When interrupting and holding the floor, it is usually most effective to combine sounds and gestures with the words and phrases.

1 Look at the cartoon and answer the questions.

1. Where are the man and the woman?

   _____

2. What is the man doing?

   _____

3. How is the woman responding to him?

   _____

2 Work with a partner. Complete the classroom discussion. Write phrases for interrupting and holding the floor. Then practice the conversation in a group of three. Switch roles and repeat.

KYOO HYUN: ... So, what are the effects of global warming? One is that cyclones are bigger and more frequent...

BRIDGET: (asking for clarification) **(1)** _____, could you repeat that?

KYOO HYUN: Cyclones. They're getting bigger and more frequent.

BRIDGET: (asking for clarification) **(2)** _____

KYOO HYUN: Yes?

BRIDGET: What's a cyclone?

KYOO HYUN: Oh, it's a really big storm that has very fast wind, like a hurricane or typhoon. As I was saying ...

SAM: (making a comment) **(3)** _____ There've been a lot of strong cyclones recently, but I think it might not be caused by global warming.

KYOO HYUN: Some people say that, but most scientists don't agree.

SAM: (making a comment) **(4)** _____ I've heard that ...

KYOO HYUN: (holding the floor) **(5)** _____. I want to finish this idea. . . .

3 Work in a small group. Discuss the question for 4 minutes. Each person should interrupt at least once to ask for clarification or make a comment. Each person should also hold the floor at least once, if interrupted. Use the Speaking Skill strategies.

Question: What can individuals, government, and industry do to reduce carbon emissions?

▪▪▪▪▪▪▪▪▪▪▪▪▪▪▪▪▪▪▪▪▪▪▪▪ GO TO MyEnglishLab FOR MORE SKILL PRACTICE AND TO CHECK WHAT YOU LEARNED.

FINAL SPEAKING TASK

In an academic seminar, there is usually a small group of students with a leader. The leader presents information to the group and leads a discussion. In this activity, each student will take turns being the leader and the other students will participate in the discussion.

In this activity, you will lead and participate in an academic seminar.

Work in a group of four or five. Follow the steps. Try to use the vocabulary, grammar, pronunciation, and listening and speaking skills that you learned in the unit.*

STEP 1: Choose a seminar topic. Each group member should choose a different topic.

- Topic A: global CO_2 emissions (Figures 1–2, page 205; discussion questions, page 205)

- Topic B: transportation (Figure 3, page 206; discussion questions, page 206)

- Topic C: natural disasters and global warming (Figure 4, page 207; discussion questions, page 207)

- Topic D: sea level rise and global warming (Figure 5, page 208; discussion questions, page 208)

STEP 2: Prepare for the seminar. You will become the expert on your topic.

- Study the information about your topic. Look at the figure and the discussion questions for your topic only. Make sure you understand all of the vocabulary.

- Think of an additional discussion question.

- You can also work with students from other groups who have the same topic.

STEP 3: With your seminar group, lead a discussion on your topic using the discussion questions. Make sure to refer to your figure during the discussion.

---

*For Alternative Speaking Topics, see page 209.

Topic A: Global CO$_2$ Emissions

A country's carbon dioxide emissions can be measured in two ways: the total amount of CO$_2$ produced by the whole country (Figure 1) or the amount of CO$_2$ produced by each person (Figure 2).

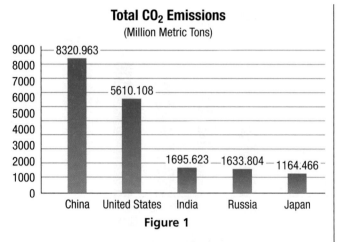

Total CO$_2$ Emissions
(Million Metric Tons)

China 8320.963
United States 5610.108
India 1695.623
Russia 1633.804
Japan 1164.466

Figure 1

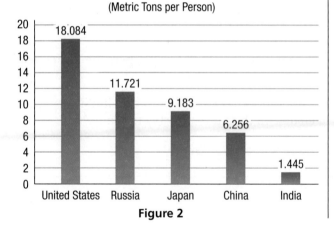

Per Person CO$_2$ Emissions
(Metric Tons per Person)

United States 18.084
Russia 11.721
Japan 9.183
China 6.256
India 1.445

Figure 2

Source: US Energy Information Administration (Data for 2010)

Discussion Questions

1. Look at Figure 1. Which countries produce the most and least total CO$_2$ emissions?

2. Look at Figure 2. Which countries produce the most and least CO$_2$ emissions per person?

3. Why do you think some countries have high total emissions but low per person emissions?

4. Do you think these countries can all lower their CO$_2$ emissions in the same way? How should their approaches be similar or different?

5. Your question: _____

_____

Topic B: Transportation

Transportation produces about 20 percent of CO_2 emissions. Cars are a major source of emissions. Figure 3 shows the number of cars per 100 people in different regions around the world.

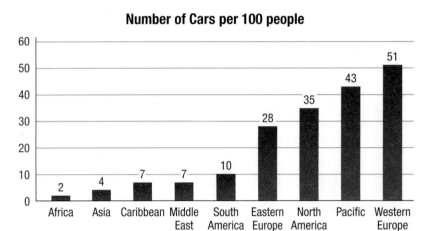

Number of Cars per 100 people

Source: Ward's Automotive Group; Population Reference Bureau (Data for 2010)

Figure 3

Discussion Questions

1. Look at Figure 3. Which areas of the world have the most cars per person? Which have the least?

2. Why do you think there is such a big difference in the number of cars in different parts of the world? Do you think that will change in the future, or stay the same?

3. How can we convince people to stop buying and driving cars?

4. Your question: _____

Topic C: Natural Disasters and Global Warming

Figure 4 shows the number of natural disasters from 1980 to 2012.

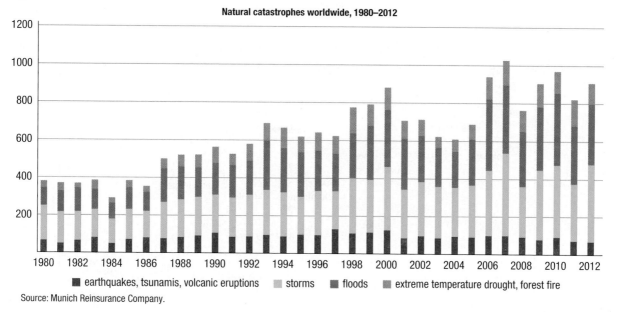

Figure 4

Discussion Questions

1. Look at Figure 4. What types of disasters have increased since 1980? What types of disasters have stayed about the same?

2. Think of a weather-related natural disaster that you have heard about or experienced. When and where did the disaster happen? What were the effects?

3. How can individuals and governments protect themselves from the effects of weather-related disasters?

4. Your question: _____

Topic D: Sea Level Rise and Global Warming

Global warming may cause ice in the North and South Poles to melt. The melted ice will cause sea levels to rise. The red areas in Figure 5 show places that will be underwater after a six-meter (19.7-foot) sea level rise.

Areas at Risk from Sea Level Rise

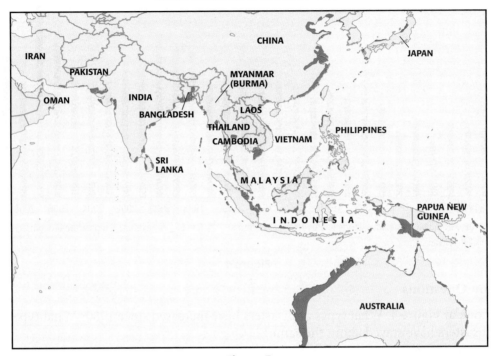

Figure 5

Source: Jeremy L. Weiss and Jonathan Overpeck. Environmental Studies Laboratory, Department of Geosciences, University of Arizona

Other places affected by six-meter rise:

Amsterdam, the Netherlands   London, England   New York, United States

Lagos, Nigeria   Miami, United States   Vancouver, Canada

Discussion Questions

1. Look at Figure 5. What do the red areas show?

2. What places will be most affected by sea level rise?

3. What will happen to the people who live in the areas close to a sea?

4. How will sea level rise affect people who do not live close to the sea?

5. Your question: _____

Listening Task

Listen and respond to the group's questions and comments during the discussion. When another person in your seminar is leading, participate actively in the discussion.

UNIT PROJECT

There are many services and technologies that can help lower carbon emissions, including:

Transportation: car sharing services (Zip Car, I-GO), hybrid electric cars, biofuel, bicycle sharing programs

Electrical use: Energy Star appliances, compact fluorescent light bulbs, wind power, solar power, hydropower

Heating and cooling: green buildings, solar heat, eco-roofs, insulation, geothermal

Business and industry: tree planting programs, CO_2 emissions trading, green product design

STEP 1: Do research on the Internet about a service or technology that reduces carbon emissions. Find out how it works, how much it costs, and how it reduces carbon emissions.

STEP 2: Share your research in a small group or with the class.

ALTERNATIVE SPEAKING TOPICS

Discuss one of the topics. Use the vocabulary and grammar from the unit.

1. How has climate change affected you or your community? Have you seen any effects of climate change? What are people doing to reduce carbon emissions? Explain.

2. What lifestyle changes could you make to reduce your own carbon footprint?

GO TO MyEnglishLab TO DISCUSS ONE OF THE ALTERNATIVE TOPICS, WATCH A VIDEO ABOUT A FAMILY LIVING THE SIMPLE LIFE, AND TAKE THE UNIT 8 ACHIEVEMENT TEST.

STUDENT ACTIVITIES

From Unit 3 Final Speaking Task, page 75

GROUP 1: Finance and Economy

- The United States spends over $18 billion a year on space exploration.
- The money spent on the United States space program is less than 1 percent of the total budget for the country.
- One dollar ($1) spent on the space program results in eight dollars ($8) of economic benefit through the creation of new jobs and new products that are sold around the world.
- The space program creates new jobs. For example, the project to send the Curiosity Rover to Mars created at least 7,000 jobs in seven years.
- Some people say that the products that have been invented through the space program might have been invented more cheaply on Earth.
- Other: _____

GROUP 2: The Environment

- Satellites in space allow us to observe environmental problems. For example, we can observe global warming (rising temperatures) by seeing the ice melting at the North Pole. We can also see pollution in the oceans and the destruction of the rainforests.
- Satellites allow us to track big storms, such as cyclones and hurricanes, as well as large fires.
- The space program has invented a process for cleaning chemicals out of water. This process is now used on Earth to take harmful chemicals out of dirty water from factories.
- When rockets travel into space, harmful chemicals are put into the air. Spacecraft also burn lot of fuel.
- Spacecraft leave orbital debris in space. These fragments can damage satellites, the International Space Station, and other spacecraft. They can also fall to Earth.
- Other: _____

GROUP 3: Innovation and Development

 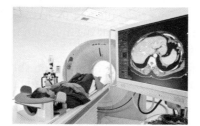 

Products created by space research

- Many high quality, innovative products have been invented as a result of the space program. Some examples are: sunglasses, paint that doesn't burn in a fire, safety systems for cars, medical equipment, and equipment to help us see at night.

- Satellite communications have changed people's lives with cell phone service, GPS navigation, and weather prediction. They have changed business with better communication, faster banking services, video conferencing, and other new technologies.
- Some products invented through the space program might have been invented more cheaply on Earth.
- Asteroids contain precious metals that we can use on Earth. Companies are working now to find a way to go into space, get metals from asteroids, and bring them back to Earth.
- Space tourism is a growing industry. There are many people who would like to travel to space as a tourist. Space tourists have already paid $20 million to $35 million to travel to the International Space Station.
- Other: _____

GROUP 4: Human Relations

- Space exploration has promoted cooperation between different countries. Russia, Japan, the European Union, China, and the United States all work together on most projects. Sixty percent of American scientific projects are performed with scientists from other countries, and all the human space flights are made in partnership with other countries.
- The International Space Station was constructed with the cooperation of many nations. Today, scientists from many countries live together on the station and do research.
- Satellite technology has brought people closer together because we can communicate more easily over long distances. International business is also easier because of global banking and communications systems.
- Countries compete with each other to be the first to do something in space. Just as the United States and the Soviet Union competed to put the first man in space, competition can create negative relationships between the countries.
- Countries use satellite technology to gather information about other countries and their own people. They use the information to make political or military decisions.
- Other: _____

TOPIC A: Global CO$_2$ Emissions

A country's carbon dioxide emissions can be measured in two ways: to show the total amount of CO$_2$ produced by the whole country (Figure 1) or the amount of CO$_2$ produced by each person (Figure 2).

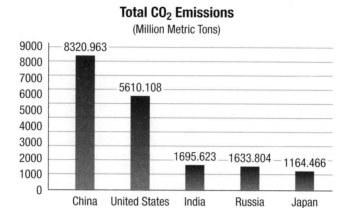

Total CO$_2$ Emissions
(Million Metric Tons)

Figure 1

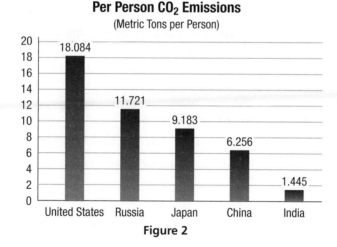

Per Person CO$_2$ Emissions
(Metric Tons per Person)

Figure 2

Source: US Energy Information Administration (Data for 2010)

Discussion Questions

1. Look at Figure 1. Which countries produce the most and least total CO$_2$ emissions?
2. Look at Figure 2. Which countries produce the most and least CO$_2$ emissions per person?
3. Why do you think some countries have high total emissions but low per person emissions?
4. Do you think these countries can all lower their CO$_2$ emissions in the same way? How should their approaches be similar or different?
5. Your question: _____

TOPIC B: Transportation

Transportation produces about 20 percent of CO_2 emissions. Cars are a major source of emissions. Figure 3 shows the number of cars per 100 people in different regions around the world.

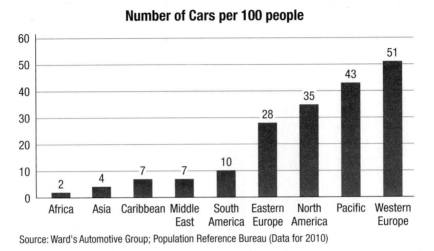

Number of Cars per 100 people

Source: Ward's Automotive Group; Population Reference Bureau (Data for 2010)

Figure 3

Discussion Questions

1. Look at Figure 3. Which areas of the world have the most cars per person? Which have the fewest?
2. Why do you think there is such a big difference in the number of cars in different parts of the world? Do you think that will change in the future or stay the same?
3. How can we convince people to stop buying and driving cars?
4. Your question: _____

TOPIC C: Climate Change and Natural Disasters

Figure 4 shows the number of natural disasters from 1980 to 2012.

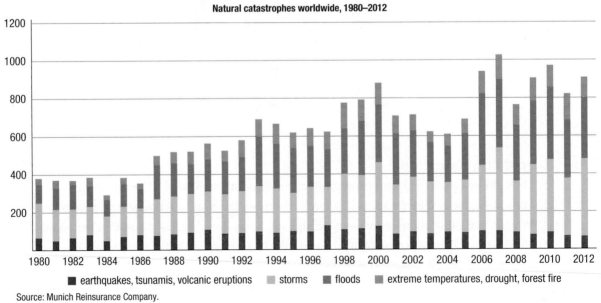

Natural catastrophes worldwide, 1980–2012

■ earthquakes, tsunamis, volcanic eruptions   storms   ■ floods   ■ extreme temperatures, drought, forest fire

Source: Munich Reinsurance Company.

Figure 4

Discussion Questions

1. Look at Figure 4. What types of disasters have increased since 1980? What types of disasters have stayed about the same?

2. Think of a weather-related natural disaster that you have heard about or experienced. When and where did the disaster happen? What were the effects?

3. How can individuals and governments protect themselves from the effects of weather-related disasters?

4. Your question: _____

TOPIC D: Sea Level Rise and Global Warming

Global warming might cause ice at the North and South Poles to melt. The melted ice will cause sea levels to rise. The red areas in Figure 5 show places that will be underwater after a 19.7-foot (6 meter) sea-level rise.

Areas at Risk from Sea Level Rise

Figure 5

Source: Jeremy L. Weiss and Jonathan Overpeck. Environmental Studies Laboratory, Department of Geosciences, University of Arizona

Other places affected by 19.7-foot sea-level rise:

Amsterdam, the Netherlands	London, England	New York, United States
Lagos, Nigeria	Miami, United States	Vancouver, Canada

Discussion Questions

1. Look at Figure 5. What do the red areas show?

2. Which places will be most affected by sea level rise?

3. What will happen to the people who live in the areas close to a sea?

4. How will sea-level rise affect people who do not live close to the sea?

5. Your question: _____

UNIT WORD LIST

The Unit Word List is a summary of key vocabulary from the Student Book.
Words followed by an asterisk* are on the Academic Word List (AWL).

UNIT 1

achieve*	motivation*
challenge*	opponent
course	ration
experience	stage
format*	tent
get into	terrain
goal*	unique*
marathon	

UNIT 2

authorize*	proof of
charge	identification
commit*	protect
confirm*	purchase*
deal with	risk
exposed*	shred
file* a	tip
complaint	victim
paranoid	

UNIT 3

collide	particle
cooperate*	perspective*
crew	precious
damage	promote*
debris	satellite
fragment	spacecraft
innovation*	track
orbit	

UNIT 4

compact	excessive
connotation	fire
context	maintenance*
corporate*	reduction
cozy	transition*
deceptive	vibrant
directly	vintage
euphemism	

UNIT 5

bribe
drop out
enroll
environment*
figure out
major*
management
process*

shift*
strategy*
supportive
take a chance
tunnel vision*
ultimately*
volunteer*

UNIT 6

afford
community*
controversy
degrading
develop
make a living
preserve
salary

season
souvenir
stretch
tourist attraction
tradition*
wrapped
zoo

UNIT 7

blow up
bother
breadwinner
budget
check up on
contract*
court
expectation

flexible*
legal*
occur*
open up
quirk
rush into
work out

UNIT 8

bed
collectively
consumption*
dense
a drop in the
   bucket
emissions
energy*-
   efficient

factory
generation*
greenhouse gas
industry
resource*
solar panel*
technology*
transport*

GRAMMAR BOOK REFERENCES

NorthStar: Listening and Speaking Level 3, Fourth Edition	Focus on Grammar Level 3, Fourth Edition	Azar's Fundamentals of English Grammar, Fourth Edition
Unit 1 Reflexive and Reciprocal Pronouns	**Unit 27** Reflexive and Reciprocal Pronouns	**Chapter 6** Nouns and Pronouns: 6-13
Unit 2 Modals of Advice	**Unit 16** Advice: *Should, Ought to, Had better*	**Chapter 7** Modal Auxiliaries: 7-7, 7-8
Unit 3 Present Perfect and Simple Past	**Unit 11** Present Perfect and Simple Past	**Chapter 4** Present Perfect and Past Perfect: 4-2, 4-8
Unit 4 Superlative Adjectives	**Unit 21** Adjectives: Superlatives	**Chapter 9** Comparisons: 9-10
Unit 5 Infinitives of Purpose	**Unit 25** More Uses of Infinitives	**Chapter 13** Gerunds and Infinitives
Unit 6 Predictions with *Will* and *If*-clauses	**Unit 6** Future	**Chapter 3** Future Time: 3-6
Unit 7 Comparatives and Equatives	**Unit 20** Adjectives: Comparisons with *As . . . as* and *Than*	**Chapter 9** Comparisons: 9-1, 9-6
Unit 8 Modals of Necessity	**Unit 29** Necessity: *Have (got) to, Must, Don't have to, Must not, Can't*	**Chapter 7** Modal Auxiliaries: 7-9, 7-10

AUDIOSCRIPT

UNIT 1: A Test of Endurance

Listening One, page 5, Preview

JAY BATCHEN: . . . I mean, you're sleeping in a tent every night, there are sandstorms, you're sharing the tent with eight other people, it's not fully enclosed, so you have wind and sand and people snoring and rustling next to you. You're sleeping on rocks.

TIM BOURQUIN: Well, you know Jay, it doesn't sound like a whole lot of fun; so, you know, in the night, you're not getting a lot of sleep. What is in it for you? What does the race do for you personally?

Page 6, Main Ideas

TIM BOURQUIN: Thank you for joining us at EnduranceRadio.com. We've got another great interview for you today. We're going to be speaking with Jay Batchen. He was the first American to finish the Marathon des Sables. We're going to hear about that and his background in ultrarunning and a little bit about his background in endurance sports in general. So, Jay, thanks very much for joining us. I appreciate you taking the time to talk to us on the phone.

JAY BATCHEN: Thank you, Tim. It's my pleasure.

TIM BOURQUIN: So, talk about the Marathon des Sables. How did you get into that?

JAY BATCHEN: It's funny how I did get into the Marathon des Sables. I was introduced to it while working for the Discovery Channel. I filmed the event in 1999, which is actually the year my wife, Lisa Smith-Batchen, won the event. And that's how I ended up in Morocco and ended up learning about the event myself.

TIM BOURQUIN: So, did you know Lisa before that event, or you met her there?

JAY BATCHEN: Met her there.

TIM BOURQUIN: OK, so you ended up marrying the winner of the race that you were filming.

JAY BATCHEN: Yep.

TIM BOURQUIN: Oh, very good. So, talk about that race. How did that start? How long is it? Where is it? That sort of thing, for our listeners that may not know.

JAY BATCHEN: Sure. The race is . . . it takes place in the Sahara Desert in southern Morocco, just outside of the Atlas Mountains. And the course is different every year. For instance, this year, it was a 154-mile course, and the year I ran it, in 2000, it was about 148 that year, so . . .

TIM BOURQUIN: Wow.

JAY BATCHEN: . . . it just changes year to year, and obviously the terrain will change as well, since the course does.

TIM BOURQUIN: Now, is this a stage race, or is it just start and go till you finish?

JAY BATCHEN: No, this particular race is a stage race, and the format is fairly, fairly similar each year in that the first three stages are all around 20 miles, give or take, and then the fourth stage is a 50-mile-long stage. Then that's followed by a full marathon. And the last day basically makes up the difference, just gets you back into a town, and it's a little shorter. Gives everyone a chance to get across the finish line and get back to the small town where we rendezvous and clean up for a nice night of awards and festivities.

TIM BOURQUIN: If you're able to stay standing at that point, I guess.

JAY BATCHEN: Definitely. And what's unique about this race is that you do have to carry all of your food, extra clothing, and things like that for the entire event. You are given a ration of water each day at checkpoints roughly about 6 to 8 miles in length. I mean, you're sleeping in a tent every night; there are sandstorms; you're sharing the tent with eight other people; it's not fully enclosed, so you have wind and sand and people snoring and rustling next to you. You're sleeping on rocks

TIM BOURQUIN: Well, you know Jay, it doesn't sound like a whole lot of fun; so, you know, in the night, you're not getting a lot of sleep. What is in it for you? What does the race do for you personally?

JAY BATCHEN: That's a good question, and it's a question that many people ask. And what I tell them is that this race is more than a race. It's a life experience. And what I mean by that is you're sharing a tent with eight other people, and you're going through the same highs and lows every day. It might not be at the same time, but you're running in the same heat, you're running in the same wind, you're sleeping in the same sandstorms on the cold nights, and for me it's about meeting the other people that are running this event and sharing stories with them and sharing the experience with them. And it's so hard to describe to someone who hasn't been there and run the event. So for me, it's completing the distance and knowing that I can do it, feeling that I can do it; but it's meeting the people from all over the world, from all walks of life, and just sharing it with them that makes it special.

Page 8, Make Inferences, 1

Excerpt One

JAY BATCHEN: . . . the format is fairly, fairly similar each year in that the first three stages are all around 20 miles, give or take, and then the fourth stage is a 50-mile-long stage. Then that's followed by a full marathon. And the last day basically makes up the difference, just gets you back into a town, and it's a little shorter. Gives everyone a chance to get across the finish line and get back to the small town where we rendezvous and clean up for a nice night of awards and festivities.

TIM BOURQUIN: If you're able to stay standing at that point, I guess.

JAY BATCHEN: Definitely.

Excerpt Two

JAY BATCHEN: I mean, you're sleeping in a tent every night; there are sandstorms; you're sharing the tent with eight other people; it's not fully enclosed, so you have wind and sand and people snoring and rustling next to you. You're sleeping on rocks.

TIM BOURQUIN: Well, you know Jay, it doesn't sound like a whole lot of fun; so, you know, in the night, you're not getting a lot of sleep.

Listening Two, page 10, Comprehension

PROFESSOR: So last time, when we were discussing the growth of endurance sports, a question came up about the motivation for getting into these sports. Why would anyone want to go through so much physical pain and stress? What's in it for them? Well, looking at the research, there are a couple points that seem especially important.

One of these is the personality of endurance athletes. As a group, these people tend to be high achievers—you know, people who set high goals for themselves, both in sports and in life in general. They like difficult challenges, and they aren't happy with goals that are easy to achieve. So endurance sports fits right into this type of personality. These sports are very difficult, very extreme—like ultramarathons where people run hundreds of miles, often in extreme heat or cold—but the athletes get a lot of satisfaction from it. And when setting goals, most endurance athletes don't focus on winning the race. Instead, they have personal goals, like maybe just finishing the race is enough, or finishing with a better time than before. So it's really more about the athletes challenging themselves, doing their personal best, and always pushing to do better.

Another source of motivation is the relationship between the athletes. In general, endurance athletes don't see the other athletes in a race as opponents, or people they're trying to beat. Instead, they see them as partners—partners in this unique adventure, doing something that no one else is doing. They share the highs and lows of the race, the pain and the pleasure, and they feel that they are in the experience together. And the athletes report this as a life-changing experience . . . an emotional high that keeps them wanting to come back for more. So this, this strong emotional experience is a big part of the motivation.

Page 12, Listening Skill, 1

PROFESSOR: Why would anyone want to go through so much physical pain and stress? What's in it for them? Well, looking at the research, there are a couple points that seem especially important.

Page 12, Listening Skill, 2

1. **PROFESSOR:** Well, looking at the research, there are a couple points that seem especially important. One of these is the personality of endurance athletes.

2. **PROFESSOR:** And when setting goals, most endurance athletes don't focus on winning the race. Instead, they have personal goals, like maybe just finishing the race is enough . . .

3. **PROFESSOR:** So it's really more about the athletes challenging themselves, doing their personal best, and always pushing to do better. Another source of motivation is the relationship between the athletes.

4. **PROFESSOR:** And the athletes report this as a life-changing experience . . . an emotional high that keeps them wanting to come back for more. So this, this strong emotional experience is a big part of the motivation.

Page 13, Connect the Listenings, Step 1: Organize

JAY BATCHEN: That's a good question, and it's a question that many people ask. And what I tell them is that this race is more than a race. It's a life experience. And what I mean by that is you're sharing a tent with eight other people, and you're going through the same highs and lows every day. It might not be at the same time, but you're running in the same heat, you're running in the same wind, you're sleeping in the same sandstorms on the cold nights, and for me it's about meeting the other people that are running this event and sharing stories with them and sharing the experience with them. And it's so hard to describe to someone who hasn't been there and run the event. So for me, it's completing the distance and knowing that I can do it, feeling that I can do it; but it's meeting the people from all over the world, from all walks of life, and just sharing it with them that makes it special.

UNIT 2: Avoiding Identity Theft

Listening One, page 32, Preview

LILY: So, by the end of the week, I was feeling totally helpless. And, like, a total victim. What do I do now? I have $30,000 worth of credit card bills in my name, with my address, and I felt really exposed. Somebody knows who I am, where I live, what my phone number is, and I'm helpless to stop this.

Page 32, Main Ideas

ANNOUNCER: Lily's wallet was stolen at a restaurant. The thief used her personal information to open credit cards in her name. But she had no idea she was the victim of identity theft. Then one day, she was home working on her computer when she got a call from a department store. In this story, Lily describes what happened next.

LILY: So, I was at the computer and the phone rang, I got this phone call, and she said, "Well, we have here that you've bought a diamond ring, so I'm just confirming the purchase because it's quite a bit of money." And I said, "Well, what is it?" And she said, "It's a $5,000 diamond ring." And I said, "No, I haven't left the house today, so I wouldn't have bought a diamond ring, and anyway, I don't go to that store, I don't go to your store anymore." And so, she said, "Well, somebody who has your name has purchased a diamond ring for $5,000." And I said, "Five thousand dollars! A diamond ring! Well, that's not me. I didn't buy it, and I don't authorize the purchase of this diamond ring, OK? So, we have a problem."

And she said, "We don't have a problem; I think, I hate to tell you this, you have a problem." And I said, "What are you talking about?" She said, "I hate to break the news to you, but I think that you have been a victim of identity theft." And I said, "A victim of what?" And she said, "Identity theft." And she said, "Well, when you get this bill . . ." And I said, "Excuse me? I'm going to get a bill for this?" She says, "Oh, yes. When you get the bill, you need to file a complaint." And I said, "Oh, boy."

So, I did that, I filed the complaint. And then, it just went from bad to worse.

On Monday, I got home from work and I checked my mail, and there was a bill from another department store and another department store. On Tuesday, there were two more bills from two other department stores. On Wednesday, there were three bills from three consumer electronics stores. On Thursday, there were

four bills from a jewelry store, a clothing store, another department store. . . . By Friday, I had accumulated close to 38 or 39 bills. And I was up to probably close to $30,000 worth of charges, if not more. So, by the end of the week, I was feeling totally helpless. And, like, a total victim. What do I do now? I have $30,000 worth of credit card bills in my name, with my address, and I felt really exposed. Somebody knows who I am, where I live, what my phone number is, and I'm helpless to stop this.

So, what did I do? Every night, I had to deal with these bills. And what you have to do, is you have to make copies of the police report, etcetera, that, you know, my wallet was stolen. You have to describe in detail what they had purchased, and you have to write a letter to every single one of these stores that charged me, explaining what had happened. And you hope that they will not keep the charges there for you.

It took about, I would say, close to four months before the whole thing died away, and just a lot of time and a lot of worry. I worried a lot.

And the paranoia hasn't left, I mean, I'm still really conscious and nervous about receipts I have. I always rip them up into many tiny little pieces. And, the other thing that is really scary is how easy it is to open up credit cards. Shocking! You can go into any store, and you can just give them your name, your address, you don't need any proof of identification, and you can open up a credit card at that particular store. They don't really check who you are. How many clerks really look at the back of your credit card and check your signature? Not many.

There's all sorts of ways that your identity can be stolen. So, I think everybody should be paranoid.

Listening Two, page 36, Comprehension

Public Service Announcement 1

COMPANY: American Bank VISA. May I help you?
VICTIM: Yes, I'm calling about my credit card bill. There's a charge for $4,000 that I know I didn't make . . .
ANNOUNCER: Think you're safe from identity theft? Think again. Every minute, 19 people in the United States have their identities stolen. However, there are things that you can do to reduce your risk. First: Get a locked mailbox. Don't let a thief steal your mail and use it to steal your identity. Second: Be careful when someone asks you for personal information. Don't give out information over the phone, by mail, or on the Internet unless you *know* who you're dealing with. To see more tips on avoiding identity theft, visit the Identity Theft Helpline . . .

Public Service Announcement 2

ANNOUNCER: Hear that sound? That's the sound of a crime being committed. Every day, criminals find personal information from papers that we throw away. It doesn't take much—a name, an address, an ID number—and the thief has all he needs to commit identity theft.

Hear that sound? That's the sound of someone protecting herself from becoming a victim of identity theft. It only takes a minute to shred papers with personal information, but it can save you years of stress and worry.

Identity theft is the number one crime in the United States, with 10 million cases reported this year. Don't become the next victim. To find out how you can stay safe, call the Identity Theft Helpline at . . .

Page 36, Listening Skill, 1

ANNOUNCER: Think you're safe from identity theft? Think again. Every minute, 19 people in the United States have their identities stolen.

UNIT 3: Why Explore Space?

Listening One, page 54, Preview

REPORTER: When NASA announced in 2011 that an old weather satellite—a six-ton piece of space junk, the size of a bus—was falling back to earth, people worried. Scientists knew when it would fall, but not where. As it turned out, it came down harmlessly in the Pacific Ocean. But this made us wonder: How much space junk is up there? And are we in danger?

Page 55, Main Ideas

REPORTER: When NASA announced in 2011 that an old weather satellite—a six-ton piece of space junk, the size of a bus—was falling back to earth, people worried. Scientists knew when it would fall, but not where. As it turned out, it came down harmlessly in the Pacific Ocean. But this made us wonder: How much space junk is up there? And are we in danger?

MICHAELA JOHNSON: Well, we call it orbital debris, not space junk.

REPORTER: That's Michaela Johnson, a scientist who studies debris in space.

MICHAELA JOHNSON: Most of it's created when satellites collide or explode. Two recent events created one third of the debris now in space: In 2007, an old Chinese satellite exploded. And in 2009, an old Russian satellite hit an active American satellite.

REPORTER: NASA tracks 21,000 large fragments—fragments more than 10 centimeters in width, or

the size a large apple. But there are 500,000 smaller fragments—the size of a grape—that we can't track. And the number of tiny particles, less than 1 centimeter, could be in the hundreds of millions. All these fragments orbit the earth in a giant debris cloud. We're looking at a map of the debris on a computer screen.

MICHAELA JOHNSON: So, this is the earth. And you see here, each dot is a piece of debris larger than 10 centimeters.

REPORTER: So far, no one has been injured or killed by space debris falling to Earth.

MICHAELA JOHNSON: Most of it burns up long before it reaches the ground. But on average, one piece of space debris falls to Earth each day—usually in the ocean or a place where no people live.

REPORTER: A bigger problem is the fragments in Earth's orbit. These fragments are dangerous because they travel incredibly fast, about 8 kilometers per second.

MICHAELA JOHNSON: That's eight times faster than a speeding bullet.

REPORTER: At that speed, even small fragments can do serious damage to a spacecraft. And with each collision, more debris is created, increasing the chances of another collision. The problem will only get worse unless we can stop the creation of more space debris. And with over 1,000 working satellites in orbit, we might all feel the effects.

MICHAELA JOHNSON: Our communication satellites, our weather satellites, our navigation satellites are all in danger.

REPORTER: That means our phone calls, TV signals, weather reports, and GPS map systems.

MICHAELA JOHNSON: And it's not just a U.S. problem, it's an international problem. Every country that sends a spacecraft or satellite into space—we're all part of the problem. So the international community needs to cooperate. We have to stop creating new debris, and to clean up the debris that's already there.

REPORTER: There is some progress. Space agencies from 12 countries have formed an organization, the Inter-Agency Space Debris Coordination Committee, to find a solution. But until then, we'll keep an eye on the sky. Just in case.

Page 57, Make Inferences, 1

Excerpt One

REPORTER: NASA tracks 21,000 large fragments—fragments more than 10 centimeters in width, or the size a large apple. But there are 500,000 smaller fragments—the size of a grape—that we can't track. And the number of tiny particles, less than 1 centimeter, could be in the hundreds of millions. All these fragments orbit the earth in a giant debris cloud.

Excerpt Two

REPORTER: So far, no one has been injured or killed by space debris falling to Earth.

MICHAELA JOHNSON: Most of it burns up long before it reaches the ground. But on average, one piece of space debris falls to Earth each day—usually in the ocean or a place where no people live.

Excerpt Three

REPORTER: A bigger problem is the fragments in Earth's orbit. These fragments are dangerous because they travel incredibly fast, about 8 kilometers per second.

MICHAELA JOHNSON: That's eight times faster than a speeding bullet.

Listening Two, page 60, Comprehension

INTERVIEWER: One criticism of the space program is the cost. The U.S. government is spending over 18 billion dollars on space exploration. Is it worth the price?

SCIENTIST: Space exploration has a lot of benefits. One is innovation. The research for the space program has led to all kinds of innovations.

INTERVIEWER: Can you tell us about some of those?

SCIENTIST: Think about it: to get into space we had to solve all kinds of problems, problems we never had on Earth, that required new ideas and solutions. And these innovations didn't just stay in space. Hundreds of new products have been created from this research—things we use on Earth every day. Let me give you some examples—water filters, used to clean water. And smoke detectors, to protect your house from fire. They were both developed for use in space.

INTERVIEWER: You've talked about other benefits, ones that can't be measured in dollars and cents. Could you describe some of those?

SCIENTIST: Well, space exploration now requires a great deal of international cooperation. For example, the International Space Station. Five different space agencies worked together to build and run the station. It's brought together international flight crews from 15 nations. The training and research, the supplies and communication networks: they're all international efforts. This cooperation promotes positive relationships between nations.

INTERVIEWER: There are other, more personal benefits as well.

SCIENTIST: Right. Since the beginning of time, we've had a great curiosity about the world around us. We've always wanted to learn more, to see more. This curiosity has led us to explore every corner of Earth. But we've only just begun in space! There is so much more that we need to find out. And it doesn't just give us answers; it gives perspective. Seeing Earth from space—a small blue planet floating in a giant black sky—we see how precious it is. And that's a perspective we should never forget.

Page 61, Listening Skill, 1

INTERVIEWER: One criticism of the space program is the cost. The U.S. government is spending over 18 billion dollars on space exploration. Is it worth the price?

Page 61, Listening Skill, 2

Excerpt One

SCIENTIST: For example, the International Space Station. Five different space agencies worked together to build and run the station. It's brought together international flight crews from 15 nations. The training and research, the supplies and communication networks, they're all international efforts. This cooperation promotes positive relationships between nations.

Excerpt Two

SCIENTIST: Right. Since the beginning of time, we've had a great curiosity about the world around us. We've always wanted to learn more, to see more. This curiosity has led us to explore every corner of Earth. But we've only just begun in space! There is so much more that we need to find out. And it doesn't just give us answers—it gives perspective. Seeing Earth from space—a small blue planet floating in a giant black sky—we see how precious it is.

UNIT 4: Words That Persuade

Listening One, page 82, Preview

LECTURER: The corporate world loves euphemism. A friend of mine got a letter from his employer that said the company was having a "workforce reduction" because of "changes in the market environment." What they really mean is that a bunch of people are going to be fired because the company is in financial trouble. So why didn't they say that directly?

Page 82, Main Ideas

LECTURER: The corporate world loves euphemism. A friend of mine got a letter from his employer that said the company was having a "workforce reduction" because of "changes in the market environment." What they really mean is that a bunch of people are going to be fired because the company is in financial trouble. So why didn't they say that directly?

Well, it was an attempt to put a happy face on a bad situation. Instead of talking about people getting fired from their jobs, the company used a euphemism to make it sound better—"workforce reduction."

We love to rename things to make them sound better. Who wants to be a garbage collector? *Garbage* has a negative connotation—dirty, smelly garbage. So now we don't have garbage collectors anymore. No, instead, we have "sanitation workers." *Sanitation* is the removal of dirt to protect public health. That's a much better connotation, focusing on cleanliness rather than dirt.

Sometimes we make ourselves look better with euphemisms. Unemployed? Out of a job? That doesn't sound good in a job interview. But don't worry, you can say you are "between jobs," implying that it is only a temporary period of unemployment. Or better yet, that you "are going through a career transition." That sounds like you made a choice to be unemployed and find a better career.

But, in other contexts, our euphemisms change. With friends, you might say something else. Have you heard the term "funemployed?" That's how my friend explains his current situation—he's out of a job, but now has the time to do fun things during the work week. "Funemployed"—sounds great, right?

And we're always inventing new euphemisms. Why? Well, most have a short shelf life ... they become less effective over time. Euphemisms are created to make an idea sound more positive. But, over time, they can take on a negative connotation, just like the original word! The term "downsizing" is an example. In the 1980s— when we first heard the term "downsizing"—it was a new way to describe a company that was firing people. ... a company coming "down in size" ... However, over the years, it's become just as bad—just like saying "we're firing people." The connotation is the same now! So it's been replaced too—with new euphemisms like "workforce reduction."

If I could give the corporate world one piece of advice, I'd tell them "Don't overdo it with euphemisms— because, with excessive use, euphemism slides into *doublespeak*." "Doublespeak" is language that goes beyond making something sound better— "Doublespeak" is deceptive language used to hide the truth. There's a well-known example—you can find it on the Internet—of a corporate letter that uses 29 different euphemisms for firing people. Twenty-nine— in one page! That's too much—people get angry at this

kind of doublespeak. They want to be told the truth, not hear euphemisms that hide the truth.

So listen to the euphemisms around you, and learn to use them wisely. Thank you.

Page 84, Make Inferences, I

Excerpt One
LECTURER: Have you heard the term "funemployed?" That's how my friend explains his current situation— he's out of a job, but now has the time to do fun things during the work week.

Excerpt Two
LECTURER: In the 1980s—when we first heard the term "downsizing"—it was a new way to describe a company that was firing people . . . . a company coming "down in size" . . . However, over the years, it's become just as bad—just like saying "we're firing people." The connotation is the same now!

Excerpt Three
LECTURER: There's a well-known example—you can find it on the Internet—of a corporate letter that uses 29 different euphemisms for firing people. Twenty-nine—in one page! That's too much—people get angry at this kind of doublespeak. They wanna be told the truth, not hear euphemisms that hide the truth.

Listening Two, page 87, Comprehension
REAL ESTATE AGENT: So let me tell you a little about this place. It's really great. It's got two bedrooms, and it's right in your price range. Let's go on in . . .

CLIENT: OK!

REAL ESTATE AGENT: This is the living room. It has some really great features. Look at the nice wood floors and the big windows.

CLIENT: It seems awfully . . . small . . . Where'd my sofa go?

REAL ESTATE AGENT: Yes, it's cozy, but I think you can work with it. I'd definitely put the sofa over here along this wall, and that would open up the space.

CLIENT: There's a lot of noise coming from the street . . .

REAL ESTATE AGENT: Yes, it's a vibrant neighborhood, lots of shops and restaurants, and very convenient to transportation . . . the subway's right down the block.

CLIENT: OK.

REAL ESTATE AGENT: Can we move on to the kitchen?

CLIENT: Sure.

REAL ESTATE AGENT: Now, this kitchen has all new appliances: new stove, new dishwasher, new fridge.

CLIENT: I love the appliances. They're great. But it's kinda small, too. Not much room to move around.

REAL ESTATE AGENT: Well, it's a compact kitchen. It's very well-organized.

CLIENT: Those cabinets are sorta old fashioned.

REAL ESTATE AGENT: Isn't that a great vintage look? That's really coming back in style.

CLIENT: I guess . . .

REAL ESTATE AGENT: And out here is the back yard . . .

CLIENT: Nice . . . but not much of a garden. No grass or anything.

REAL ESTATE AGENT: Well, it's very low maintenance. You don't have to worry about mowing the grass. Add some nice planters, some flowers, it'll look great! . . . Ready to go upstairs and see the bedrooms?

CLIENT: Actually, I don't need to see any more. It's got some nice features, but it's just not gonna work for me.

REAL ESTATE AGENT: OK, no problem! I've got lots of other places to show you.

Page 88, Listening Skill, 1

So let me tell you a little about this place. It's really great.

Page 88, Listening Skill, 2

Excerpt One

This is the living room. It has some really great features.

Excerpt Two

It seems awfully small.

Excerpt Three

I'd definitely put the sofa over here along this wall, and that would open up the space.

Excerpt Four

I love the appliances. They're great. But it's kinda small, too.

UNIT 5: Follow Your Passion

Listening One, page 108, Preview

JULIE: . . . My dad is the first person that ever told me to follow your passion, and, make, you know, make money off of it. And I've always, you know, I know that's a huge phrase right now, you hear that all the time, but I heard that from my dad a long time ago.

SIMON: And I never fought so much with my parents than during this time. And I remember my parents tried everything, you know: They played good cop, bad cop. They tried bribing me. They tried saying, "We're your parents, and you're going to do this."

Page 108, Main Ideas

HOST: Erik Michaelson talked with two professionals to find out how their parents influenced their career choices. Julie Hession is a cookbook writer and the founder of a company that makes breakfast cereal.

ERIK: What role has your family played in shaping your career aspirations?

JULIE: I have a very supportive family. My dad is the first person that ever told me to follow your passion, and, make, you know, make money off of it. And I've always, you know, I know that's a huge phrase right now, you hear that all the time, but I heard that from my dad a long time ago.

ERIK: After majoring in hotel and restaurant management in college, what made you decide to shift away from that in your career?

JULIE: Well, the fact that, about three months into my first job out of college, I decided that I hated hotel and restaurant management, that was my first clue. And it was interesting because, you know, when you're an undergrad, and you're taking four years in this, in this curriculum, and all you're learning about is, you know, hotel restaurant management, hotel restaurant law, hotel restaurant marketing. . . . So I kind of had tunnel vision, and I was thinking, well this is what I've chosen to do, I'm tied to it. This is going to be my life. And I got my first job with Wyndam Hotels. They don't tell you where they're going to put you when they hire you. . . . So anyway, I got the job with Wyndam. They put me in Annapolis, Maryland, which I had, you know, great city, but I had no friends there. You didn't really make a lot of friends working in this small hotel in the city, and I was just . . . I was so unhappy, I know, I wasn't happy at work, I wasn't happy with what I was doing, and this was an instance where my dad came down to Annapolis. He drove down to Annapolis, took me to lunch. And he said, "You know, this isn't right for you. But I think you need to figure out what you want to do, and make a change, and figure out how you're going to get there." So that was, like, such an ah-ha moment for me, that I could do something else than my major! I didn't have to do my major! So that was huge, because then I started just kind of looking around, and, I think, kind of opening my mind a little bit.

HOST: Simon Sinek is an author and public speaker who studied in England and now teaches leaders and organizations how to inspire people.

ERIK: Where has your family been most supportive in your career development?

SIMON: When I graduated college, I went to law school. And after not quite a year of law school, I realized that I didn't want to be a lawyer. And so I decided that I was going to drop out of law school. And I never fought so much with my parents than during this time. And

I remember my parents tried everything, you know: They played good cop, bad cop. They tried bribing me. They tried saying, "We're your parents, and you're going to do this." They tried being my friend, like "Look, just get your law degree, then you can do anything you want." You know, I mean, every strategy that exists, they tried, right? And at the time, I wanted to go into marketing, right? I was . . . I wanted to into, to join the ad world, right? And my dad was in England on a business trip, about the time that I had to re-enroll, and he sits down with me and he says, "So?" And I remember it, I remember sitting in our friend's house, and he says to me, "So?" And I said, "I didn't re-enroll." And the first words out of his mouth were, "Right. Let's get you into advertising then." My parents were 100 percent against me until the decision was made, and then after that point, they were 100 percent supportive. And never, ever, ever raised it ever again. They literally never mentioned it again. And so I have to say, my, my, I've been very lucky in my life, which is my parents will give advice, my parents will give strong advice, my parents will try and push and move, you know, where they would like their children to go, but ultimately once the kids have made the decision, they're 100 percent supportive. And so I've been very lucky.

Page 110, Make Inferences, 1

Excerpt One

JULIE: So I kind of had tunnel vision, and I was thinking, well this is what I've chosen to do, I'm tied to it. This is going to be my life.

Excerpt Two

JULIE: And he said, "You know, this isn't right for you. But I think you need to figure out what you want to do, and make a change, and figure out how you're going to get there." So that was, like, such an ah-ha moment for me, that I could do something else than my major! I didn't have to do my major!

Excerpt Three

SIMON: When I graduated college, I went to Law School and after not quite a year of law school, I realized that I didn't want to be a lawyer. And so I decided that I was going to drop out of law school. And I never fought so much with my parents than during this time.

Excerpt Four

SIMON: My dad was in England on a business trip, about the time that I had to re-enroll, and he sits down with me and he says, "So?" And I remember it, I remember sitting in our friend's house, and he says to me, "So?"

Listening Two, page 112, Comprehension

JEREMY BENZEN: Just out of college—with a degree in biology—I got a job as a research assistant in a biotech company. Now, this was a "good job"—the pay was good and I had the chance to move up—but after a while, I realized that I didn't want to get up in the morning and go to work. I had to figure out what my real passion was. And that's what I want to talk to you about today: Finding your passion.

So first, I want to you to ask yourself, "What am I good at?" Think about skills that come easily to you, like maybe you're very artistic. Or, maybe you're good at building things. Also think about areas where other people think you're an expert. In my case, I've always loved science. And in high school, my friends always asked me for help with their science homework.

The next thing is to think about all the things you like to do. Do you love making dinner for your friends? What were your favorite classes in school? What do you do in your free time? Me, I've always liked helping people. Starting in college, I volunteered for the Red Cross, helping people in disasters or after fires. I get a lot of satisfaction from that.

My final suggestion is to make a list of the things that are important to you. What kind of environment do you want to work in? Do you want to work with your hands? Do you want a job where you can travel? As a research assistant, I mostly worked alone. But when I thought about it, I realized that I really like working with people.

So I went through this process. I looked at my scientific skills, my desire to help people, and my love of working with people, and decided that nursing was the perfect career for me. I quit my job and went back to school, and now I'm a nurse at Children's Hospital. And guess what? I love it. I took a chance, and it paid off. And that's how I found my passion in life. Thank you.

Page 114, Listening Skill, 2

A: What are you doing after college?

B: I'm going to look for a job. But there's a problem. I'm a business major, but I want to be a teacher. I should have gotten a teaching certificate. Do you think I could get a teaching job?

A: I think you should try. There's no rule that says you have to get a job that matches your major.

B: You're right. I've got to think about this some more.

UNIT 6: Culture and Commerce

Listening One, page 132, Preview

REPORTER: Each year around 10,000 tourists visit three small villages along the Thai / Myanmar border to see the famous long-necked women. The attraction is a tradition that requires women to stretch their necks by wearing brass coils. Originally from the Padaung tribe, the women and their families came from Myanmar to Thailand in the 1980s to escape poverty and war. Their new lives are very different from their lives as farmers in Myanmar. Now they make a living talking with tourists, posing for pictures, and selling handmade souvenirs.

Page 132, Main Ideas

RADIO ANNOUNCER: Critics call it "a human zoo." Tour companies consider it a tourist attraction. Whichever the case, the long-necked women of Padaung have become an important source of money for several small villages on the border of Thailand and Myanmar. Reporter Mike Danforth has this report.

TOUR LEADER: Welcome to Nai Soi. Please buy your ticket here.

REPORTER: Each year around 10,000 tourists visit three small villages along the Thai / Myanmar border to see the famous long-necked women. The attraction is a tradition that requires women to stretch their necks by wearing brass coils. Originally from the Padaung tribe, the women and their families came from Myanmar to Thailand in the 1980s to escape poverty and war. Their new lives are very different from their lives as farmers in Myanmar. Now they make a living talking with tourists, posing for pictures, and selling handmade souvenirs.

When a Padaung girl turns five, a thick coil of brass is wrapped around her neck. Throughout her life, more coils are added until her neck carries up to 25 brass rings, weighing up to 22 pounds. The coils push up her chin and press down her collarbone, making her neck longer. Pa Peiy, a young woman with 20 neck rings, describes her early years of neck stretching:

PA PEIY: At first it was painful, but now it's OK. Now sleeping, eating, working . . . everything is OK, but I cannot take it off . . . so this is my life.

REPORTER: It truly *is* her life. Pa Peiy's neck is now so weak that if she takes off the coils, her head will fall forward, and she'll stop breathing. Despite the discomfort, Padaung women in Thailand continue to wear the coils even though the tradition has almost disappeared in Myanmar. Why? Because there's money in it. Ma Nang, a graceful woman with 24 neck rings explains:

MA NANG: In Myanmar, I worked hard growing food. Now I sit, and tourists take pictures. In one month I get $70 to $80. It's easy, and it's good money for my family. Sometimes I'm tired of tourists always looking . . . but it's good money.

REPORTER: Each year, as the long-necked women have become more and more popular, the controversy about them has increased. In an outdoor restaurant near Nai Soi, tourists discuss whether or not to visit the village. Sandra, a Canadian woman, feels that it's fine to visit.

SANDRA: I don't really see a problem. I mean this is their tradition . . . and so if I go, it's like I'm helping them to preserve it. Spending my money is also helping them. You know, they make a living from tourism, so they need us.

REPORTER: Fredrick, from Germany, feels differently.

FREDRICK: Actually, I don't see that we're preserving tradition at all. This tradition has died in Myanmar already. These women are just hurting their bodies to entertain us. It's like paying to go see animals in a zoo. It's degrading.

REPORTER: For now, the future of the long-necked women is easy to predict. As long as there are tourists who will pay to see them, they will continue to wrap their daughters' necks. The controversy continues, with one side seeing the villages as examples of how tourism can save dying traditions, and others criticizing it as harmful and degrading to the Padaung women.

Page 135, Make Inferences, 1

Excerpt One

REPORTER: Originally from the Padaung tribe, the women and their families came from Myanmar to Thailand in the 1980s to escape poverty and war. Their new lives are very different from their lives as farmers in Myanmar. Now they make a living talking with tourists, posing for pictures, and selling handmade souvenirs.

Excerpt Two

FREDRICK: These women are just hurting their bodies to entertain us. It's like paying to go see animals in a zoo. It's degrading.

Listening Two, page 137, Comprehension

MAYOR: OK. We're here today to talk about tourism in our community. Let's start with the first item on our agenda—identifying some of the problems caused by the increasing number of tourists we get every year.

WOMAN 1: Well, for one, the traffic is just terrible in the summer! In winter, it takes me about 15 minutes to drive into town. But in the summer, it can be 45 minutes or more. It's ridiculous!

MAN 1: I agree, traffic gets bad, but in my mind, the biggest problem is housing. The cost of buying or renting a home here is way too high! Yeah! It's just too expensive on a regular salary. Too many homes are sold as vacation homes for rich people. And that leaves nothing for the working people who live here. I mean I own a seafood restaurant, OK? And I've got a waitress who's living in her car right now because she can't afford any other place to live. We've got to do something about that!

WOMAN 2: Can I say something? OK, I know it's difficult to have all these tourists around during the summer, but I, for one, am very happy to have them. I run a souvenir shop, and I do about 80 percent of my business for the year in the summer. And I'm not the only one. Tourists are the lifeblood of our community. Without them, I wouldn't be able to make a living. We've got to keep them coming.

MAN 2: Of course we need the tourists, no one's denying that. But I'm a business owner, too, and one problem I see is that we depend on the weather so much. When it rains, tourists don't come, huh? This season has been really difficult for my business 'cause of that. With all this rain last month, I lost a lot of money because people weren't coming in the door. I'd like to see us develop where we don't depend on the weather so much.

MAYOR: OK, before we move on, I'd like to address one of the comments made here . . .

Page 138, Listening Skill, I

MAN 1: I agree, traffic gets bad, but in my mind, the biggest problem is housing. The cost of buying or renting a home here is way too high.

Page 138, Listening Skill, 2

Excerpt One

WOMAN 2: OK, I know it's difficult to have all these tourists around during the summer, but I, for one, am very happy to have them.

Excerpt Two

MAN 2: But I'm a business owner, too, and one problem I see is that we depend on the weather so much.

Excerpt Three

MAN 2: I'd like to see us develop where we don't depend on the weather so much.

UNIT 7: Before You Say "I Do"

Listening One, page 158, Preview

HOST: Welcome to *Living Today,* the show that examines modern day issues that touch our daily lives. Today we'll be talking about marriage and how to prepare for that big step of actually tying the knot. When most couples marry, they discuss some important issues in advance, like how many children they want or where they want to live, but most of the day-to-day details and problems of married life are worked out after the wedding. Not so with my guests today, Steve and Karen Parsons, who have a 15-page marriage contract that states the rules they must follow in almost every aspect of their married life. So, Steve, Karen, welcome to the show.

Page 158, Main Ideas

HOST: Welcome to *Living Today,* the show that examines modern day issues that touch our daily lives. Today we'll be talking about marriage and how to prepare for that big step of actually tying the knot. When most couples marry, they discuss some important issues in advance, like how many children they want or where they want to live, but most of the day-to-day details and problems of married life are worked out after the wedding. Not so with my guests today, Steve and Karen Parsons, who have a 15-page marriage contract that states the rules they must follow in almost every aspect of their married life. So, Steve, Karen, welcome to the show.

STEVE: Thanks.

KAREN: Nice to be here.

HOST: So, I'd like to start off by asking you what everybody is probably wondering: Why did you decide to write this agreement? I mean, you've both been married before, am I right?

STEVE: Yeah. I've been married twice, and Karen was married once before.

KAREN: And so we have some experience about what goes wrong in a marriage.

STEVE: Right.

HOST: OK. And that's why you wrote this contract?

KAREN: Right.

STEVE: Yes, we found that most problems happen because the spouses have different expectations about the marriage. We wanted to talk about everything openly and honestly, you know, before we started living together.

KAREN: Yeah. For example, everyone has their quirks, and we're all bothered by things that might not seem important to someone else.

STEVE: Yeah.

KAREN: Like, it used to really bother me when my ex-husband left his dirty clothes on the floor, so we put that in the contract: "Dirty clothing must be put in the laundry bag." And now Steve knows what my expectations are . . .

STEVE: I'll say.

KAREN: . . . and he won't be leaving *his* clothes on the floor, right sweetie?

STEVE: Right.

HOST: Well, I'm sure that some people hearing this report will think that this isn't very romantic.

STEVE: Oh no. We disagree.

KAREN: Actually, we think it's very romantic.

STEVE: Yeah. It shows that we sat down and talked and really tried to understand each other. A lot of problems occur in a marriage because people don't open up and talk about what they want.

KAREN: That's so true! Now, when we disagree about something, we work out a compromise that's good for both of us. You know, I'd much rather do that than get some "romantic" gift like flowers or candy.

HOST: OK, so . . . I have to say some of these rules sound like . . . like, well, a business agreement. Many of them concern money in some way . . .

STEVE: Yeah.

HOST: Even the ones about having children. Let's see. Right here, you say: "After our first child is born, the partner who makes less money will quit his or her job and stay home with the child."

KAREN: Right.

HOST: Well now, that's an interesting way to decide who will do the childcare!

STEVE: Yeah, it's unusual, but it really makes sense. We definitely want someone home with our kids . . .

KAREN: Oh yeah.

STEVE: And if Karen is the main breadwinner at that point, why should she stop working? It'll be better for all of us if I stay home.

KAREN: Yeah. And the reason that we put in so many rules about money is that, in our experience, a lot of problems are caused by arguments about money.

STEVE: Oh yeah.

KAREN: So we decided to make a budget every year. And we put that in the contract, too.

HOST: Hmm, well, I'm curious, do you spend a lot of time checking up on each other to see if the rules are being followed?

KAREN: No, not at all. And we don't argue about them, either.

STEVE: No. As a matter of fact, I think we spend less time arguing than most couples because we both know what the other person expects.

KAREN: Yeah, and we can spend our time doing things we enjoy and just being with each other.

HOST: What happens if one of you breaks a rule?

STEVE: So far, that hasn't been a problem.

KAREN: Nope. Hasn't happened.

STEVE: Because we've agreed on them already.

HOST: But what if, say . . . alright, here it says "Karen will cook the meals . . ." What if you don't want to cook dinner one night? What happens?

STEVE: Well, we'll work something out. Maybe there's a good reason, like she's sick or something. We can still be flexible.

HOST: OK. But what if it happens all the time?

KAREN: Well, then we have to ask: Is this marriage really working?

STEVE: Yeah.

KAREN: Because, let's face it, if we can't follow our own agreement, there's no point.

HOST: Very true. So it sounds like you two are happy with this contract.

STEVE AND KAREN: Oh yeah.

HOST: Now let me ask you, do you think other couples should follow your example, and write marriage contracts of their own?

STEVE: Well, it's a lot of work to write something like this . . .

KAREN: That's for sure.

STEVE: . . . but I think it could be useful to a lot of people.

KAREN: Yeah, and you know, I bet there'd be fewer divorces.

HOST: OK, well look, I know we have a lot of people waiting to get in on this discussion, so let's go to some calls. Hi, you're on the air. What do you think?

Page 160, Make Inferences, 1

Excerpt One

HOST: Well, I'm sure that some people hearing this report will think that this isn't very romantic.

Excerpt Two

STEVE: Yeah, it's unusual, but it really makes sense. We definitely want someone home with our kids . . . .

Excerpt Three

STEVE: Well, it's a lot of work to write something like this . . . but I think it could be useful to a lot of people.

Listening Two, page 162, Comprehension

CALLER 1: I'm glad you guys are happy, but I'd never sign a prenuptial agreement like this. No way. I don't care what you say; it's just not very romantic. I mean if you really love someone, you don't need to write all these things down. You just need to learn how to make your spouse happy, and you've got to work out your problems right when they come up.

CALLER 2: I don't know about all this. It might be a good idea, but the main problem is this contract has way too many details. Like the rule about going to sleep at 11:00 P.M. What if one person wasn't sleepy or wanted to watch the news or something? That would be breaking a rule, right? It's crazy. You can't plan every detail in your life. That's ridiculous!

CALLER 3: Well, I think it's a great idea! You know what? I bet there'd be a lot fewer divorces if everyone did this. Most couples don't know how to open up and talk about their problems. We've all seen it, right? They let small things bother them, and they may or may not say anything at the time, and then they finally blow up and have a big fight. And then the problem gets worse because they don't know how to say "I'm sorry" afterwards. I think a contract like this could be a really helpful way to teach couples how to talk about their problems.

CALLER 4: I'm a lawyer, and I can tell you that this prenuptial agreement isn't a legal contract. It may look legal and everything, but it wouldn't hold up in court. Let's say a guy has a problem with his wife and he goes to court and he says, "I want a divorce because my wife didn't cook dinner." Well, the judge wouldn't give him a divorce for that, would he? No way! So, legally, this contract is just a bunch of words. It has no power.

CALLER 5: Yeah. I know a lot of people might think that this contract idea is crazy, but I think, I think it could be useful to help couples decide if they really *should* get married. I mean, a lot of couples, when they get married they do it, you know, because they're all in love with the other person and so on. But they don't look carefully at who the person is, really. I mean, they rush into things without thinking. And I think this contract would make both people think a lot more carefully about their expectations and, you know, if marriage is the right thing to do.

Page 163, Listening Skill, 1

CALLER 4: . . . This prenuptial agreement isn't a legal contract. It may look legal and everything, but it wouldn't hold up in court.

Page 163, Listening Skill, 2

Excerpt One

CALLER 1: I'm glad you guys are happy, but I'd never sign a prenuptial agreement like this.

Excerpt Two

CALLER 2: I don't know about all this. It might be a good idea, but the main problem is this contract has way too many details.

Excerpt Three

CALLER 4: I'm a lawyer, and I can tell you this prenuptial agreement isn't a legal contract. It may look legal and everything, but it wouldn't hold up in court.

UNIT 8: Reducing Your Carbon Footprint

Listening One, page 185, Preview

JULIA: My name is Julia Peters and I live in Portland, Oregon. It's important for me to live with a small personal carbon footprint because I realize that there are lots of people sharing this earth, and lots of people that will come after us. It's my responsibility to protect it and make it better, to live as small as I can, so that it doesn't affect future generations . . .

Page 186, Main Ideas

JULIA: Hey, come on in! Welcome to my house!

My name is Julia Peters. And I live in Portland, Oregon. It's important to me to live with a small personal carbon footprint because I realize that there are lots of people sharing this earth, and lots of people that will come after us. It's my responsibility to protect it and make it better, to live as small as I can, so that it doesn't affect future generations, their ability to live well and healthily on the planet.

We're in my house today, which is a small house, but we try to do the most with what we have. Our yard is almost all used for growing food . . . So, you have to make your way through the jungle here . . . Here in the backyard, you can see, it's not much of a yard. There's not much grass. We've taken out most of the grass to put in raised beds so that we can grow more of our own food. Right now, with it being spring, early summer, we have a lot of things that we grew from seeds inside the house, but if you were here in August and September, hopefully this would be really full with lots of tomatoes, basil plants, squash, all kinds of things.

We try to grow as much of our own food as we can because it reduces our carbon footprint. If we grow it on our own property, we don't have to go to the store and get it, and then the store buys it from someplace. For the average American, food on your plate has traveled 1,500 miles. That, obviously, is a huge environmental impact, when your food gets transported from so far away.

We also have chickens, as a way to reduce our impact. We eat mostly vegetarian. A lot of our protein comes from beans, but also from eggs. We have six chickens. "Hi, girls!" . . . They lay eggs, and in the summertime, they lay more, so right now we get about four eggs a day.

Another thing that we try to do on-site is to create our own energy. We have solar panels on our roof, and in the summertime, they produce about enough energy to power our house. Obviously, energy that doesn't come from our solar panels, we have to get from an energy company. But a lot of power in the United States comes from coal, and coal has a huge environmental impact. If we don't reduce our coal consumption, the average temperature of the earth will go up by one to two degrees, so it's a really critical time to think about how we get our power.

Our house is a small house. It has three small bedrooms, and we have four people living here. And that's another way we try to reduce our footprint, is by dense living. If I were going to live in this house by myself, I would still use energy for the lights, to heat it, to run the refrigerator. By having four people, we are collectively using almost the same amount of energy, but it's split by four people, instead of each person living in their own apartment or house. By sharing more, by living together and sharing resources, that's another way we try to reduce our footprint and limit what we use.

For some people to say that small, personal efforts are just a drop in the bucket, that they don't really have an effect, I can understand that, that makes sense. That how does one person out of 6 billion have an impact. And I think there are a few things about that to remember, is that the more people that do it, it's not just one drop, it's a lot of drops, and that can make a change.

Page 188, Make Inferences, 1

Excerpt One

JULIA: We try to grow as much of our own food as we can because it reduces our carbon footprint. If we grow it on our own property, we don't have to go to the store and get it, and then the store buys it from someplace. For the average American, food on your plate has traveled 1,500 miles.

Excerpt Two

JULIA: Our house is a small house. It has three small bedrooms, and we have four people living here. And that's another way we try to reduce our footprint, is by dense living. If I were going to live in this house by myself, I would still use energy for the lights, to heat it, to run the refrigerator. By having four people, we are collectively using almost the same amount of energy, but it's split by four people, instead of each person living in their own apartment or house.

Listening Two, page 190, Comprehension

SPEAKER: We are here today because we want to stop global warming. Like me, you're trying hard to reduce your own personal carbon footprint. And these small, individual changes do have an impact, do help lower our carbon emissions.

But it's not enough. It's not enough for individuals to change. We need governments to change. We need industry to change. We need big changes if we want to stop global warming from destroying our planet.

One third . . . one third of our global carbon emissions—35 percent—comes from producing electricity. We need government and industry to work together to lower these emissions. To develop new, cleaner technology to heat our homes, power our factories, and to keep the lights on.

Another 20 percent—20 percent!—of our emissions comes from transportation. We need government and industry to work together to build more energy-efficient cars and trucks. To build more public transportation. Good quality public transportation that will let us get rid of our cars and the pollution they produce forever!

Another 20 percent of all emissions comes from industry—our factories and businesses. Putting tons upon tons of carbon into the air —our air—every single minute. It's time to say enough! We need these businesses to lower their own personal carbon footprints!

So my message to you today is: Keep trying to reduce your personal carbon footprint. But also stand up, stand up and demand . . . demand that government and industry do their part. Because that is what will really make a difference!

Page 191, Listening Skill, 1

SPEAKER: But also stand up, stand up and demand . . . demand that government and industry do their part.

Page 191, Listening Skill, 2

Excerpt One

SPEAKER: We need government and industry to work together to lower these emissions. To develop new, cleaner technology to heat our homes, power our factories, and to keep the lights on.

Excerpt Two

SPEAKER: We need government and industry to work together to build more energy-efficient cars and trucks. To build more public transportation.

TEXT CREDITS

UNIT 1
"Extreme Running," courtesy of Tim Bourquin

UNIT 2
"Phising," http://creativecommons.org/licenses/by/3.0/

UNIT 5
"College and Career Mythis and Facts," from the "Capture Your Flag" Career Documentary Interview Series by Capture Your Flag, LLC.

UNIT 7
"Marriage Contract." D'Vera Cohn, "Love and Marriage." Pew Research Social & Demographic Trends, Washington, D.C. (February 13, 2013). http://www.pewsocialtrends.org

PHOTO CREDITS

Cover photo credits: (top left) Blend Images/Alamy, (top right) Bruce Rolff/Shutterstock, (middle left) tonyno/Fotolia, (middle right) Bruce Rolff/Shutterstock, (bottom left) Hiya Images/Corbis, (bottom right) Tan Lian Hock/AGE Fotostock.

Page xii (top) ABC News; p. 2 PIERRE VERDY/AFP/Getty Images/Newscom; p. 4 PIERRE VERDY/AFP/Getty Images; p. 10 (left) ALBERTO ESTÉVEZ/EFE/Newscom, (middle) Sebastian Rothe/Westend61 GmbH/Newscom, (right) Martin Castellan/Alamy; p. 18 Lisette Le Bon/Purestock/SuperStock; p. 24 (A) Ronnie Kaufman/Cusp/Corbis, (B) Spencer Grant/Science Source, (C) Tony Freeman/PhotoEdit, (D) Bob Thomas/Bob Thomas Sports Photography/Getty Images; p. 26 Joggie Botma/Fotolia; p. 28 Comnet/Glow Images; p. 30 Alberto Ruggieri/Illustration Works/Motif/Corbis; p. 32 Lucky Business/Shutterstock; p. 36 MIXA/Getty Images; p. 42 Jupiterimages/Creatas/Thinkstock/Getty Images; p. 50 PF-(space1)/Alamy; p. 52 Douglas Pulsipher/Alamy; p. 54 (left) JSC/NASA, (right) SCIENCE SOURCE/Photo Researchers/Getty Images; p. 59 (top) Mateusz Zajac/Fotolia, (bottom) Nikonaft/Shutterstock; p. 68 benchart/Fotolia; p. 78 Bruce Ayres/The Image Bank/Getty Images; p. 80 robhainer/Fotolia; p. 96 (top) Iriana Shiyan/Fotolia, (middle) virtua73/Fotolia, (bottom) pics721/Shutterstock; p. 98 Sergios/Fotolia; p. 99 (A) CoolR/Shutterstock, (B) Veronique Beranger/Digital Vision/Getty Images; p. 100 (C) carla9/Fotolia, (D) Jasmin Merdan/Fotolia, (E) Sozaijiten/Pearson Education, (F) Paul Maguire/Fotolia; p. 104 RubberBall/Alamy; p. 108 (left) Tetra Images/Alamy, (right) Chuck Savage/Corbis/Glow Images; p. 113 (left) Michael Ventura/Alamy, (right) RTimages/Fotolia; p. 128 Keren Su/Corbis; p. 130 Anup Shah/Nature Picture Library; p. 149 (top) Tilo Grellmann/Fotolia, (bottom) rb_fact/Fotolia; p. 154 Michael Ireland/Fotolia; p. 158 Dennis MacDonald/Alamy; p. 159 anzeletti/Getty Images; p. 162 (1) bst2012/Fotolia, (2) Goodshoot/Thinkstock/Getty Images, (3) Juanmonino/E+/Getty Images, (4) Minerva Studio/Shutterstock, (5) Lisa F. Young/Fotolia; p. 167 iofoto/Shutterstock; p. 180 Bruce Rolff/Shutterstock; p. 182 (top) manfredxy/Fotolia, (bottom) PiLensPhoto/Fotolia; p. 183 Pedro Antonio Salaverria Calahorra/Alamy; p. 185 Courtesy of Julia Peters; p. 190 Louie Balukoff/AP Images.

THE PHONETIC ALPHABET

Consonant Symbols				
/b/	be	/t/	to	
/d/	do	/v/	van	
/f/	father	/w/	will	
/g/	get	/y/	yes	
/h/	he	/z/	zoo, busy	
/k/	keep, can	/θ/	thanks	
/l/	let	/ð/	then	
/m/	may	/ʃ/	she	
/n/	no	/ʒ/	vision, Asia	
/p/	pen	/tʃ/	child	
/r/	rain	/dʒ/	join	
/s/	so, circle	/ŋ/	long	

Vowel Symbols				
/ɑ/	far, hot	/iy/	we, mean, feet	
/ɛ/	met, said	/ey/	day, late, rain	
/ɔ/	tall, bought	/ow/	go, low, coat	
/ə/	son, under	/uw/	too, blue	
/æ/	cat	/ay/	time, buy	
/ɪ/	ship	/aw/	house, now	
/ʊ/	good, could, put	/oy/	boy, coin	